This book is to be returned on or before
the last date stamped below.

WITHDRAWN
FROM
LEARNING RESOURCES
CENTRE
KINGSTON COLLEGE

D0184719

THE SHELL GUIDE TO
BRITAIN'S
THREATENED
WILDLIFE

In memory of my mother and father

THE SHELL GUIDE TO

BRITAIN'S THREATENED WILDLIFE

by Nigel Sitwell

LIBRARY

COLLINS
8 Grafton Street, London W1

First published in 1984 by William Collins Sons & Company Limited
London • Glasgow • Sydney • Auckland • Toronto • Johannesburg

Designed and produced by Threshold Books Limited,
661 Fulham Road, London SW6 5PZ

© 1984 Text Nigel Sitwell
© 1984 Design and production Threshold Books Limited
© 1984 This edition William Collins Sons & Company Limited
All rights reserved

Editor   Barbara Cooper
Designer   Alan Hamp
Editorial Assistant   Helen Gunn

Although sponsoring this book,
Shell UK Limited would point out that
the author is expressing his own views.

ISBN 0 00 219050 8

Typeset by Phoenix Photosetting, Chatham, Kent
Printed and bound in Spain by Graficromo S.A.

Acc. No.	37017
Class No.	S74 591·042
Date Rec.	17·12·84
Order No.	815261

Contents

Author's Acknowledgements

Many people have helped in the production of this book, with advice and information and in other ways. In particular I would like to thank Kevin Baker, Leo Batten, Mark Clements, Keith Corbett, Michael Everett, Lynne Farrell, Don Jeffries, Richard Pankhurst, Jean Ross, Tim Sands, Bob Stebbings, Alan Stubbs, Chris Tydeman, and Paul Whalley. In all cases their advice was supplied in a personal capacity, and does not necessarily reflect the views or policies of the organisations that they work for; I take full responsibility for the interpretation of their information. I hope that those whom I may have overlooked will forgive omission of their names caused by lack of space and an uncertain memory. I can assure them that their help was greatly valued.

I am grateful to the staffs of the British Herbarium and the Zoology Library at the Natural History Museum, and of the library at the Zoological Society of London, who were all unfailingly courteous and helpful.

I made use of many books and other published material in the course of my research, of which the most important are listed in the Bibliography. However, I must make special mention of four books on which I relied heavily, and which I can recommend to anyone with a serious interest in the conservation of our wildlife and countryside. The first is the British Red Data book on *Vascular Plants,* compiled by Franklyn Perring and Lynne Farrell, based on information supplied by members of the Botanical Society of the British Isles. It contains details of the current distribution and status of our rare plants which are available nowhere else.

The three other books are Richard Body's *Agriculture: The Triumph and the Shame,* Richard Mabey's *The Common Ground,* and Marion Shoard's *The Theft of the Countryside.* We all owe a debt of gratitude to these authors for the facts and figures which they have gathered, and their perceptive analyses of what is happening to our natural heritage.

I would like to thank a most important group of people – the individual photographers and agents, and in particular Bruce Coleman, for helping us to track down the often hard-to-find photographs on which much of the appeal of this book depends.

Acknowledgements of a different kind are due to the many organisations involved with wildlife and countryside conservation. I would like to single out the Nature Conservancy Council – our under-financed official conservation watchdog – and, on the voluntary side, the Royal Society for Conservation of Nature, together with the affiliated county trusts; the Royal Society for the Protection of Birds, and the World Wildlife Fund. They and other bodies too numerous to mention deserve our fullest support for their dedicated and vital work.

Finally, I must thank Shell UK Limited, whose sponsorship helped to make the publication of this book possible, and, above all, Barbara Cooper of Threshold Books for her dogged and good-humoured determination to see the whole project through to fruition in the face of a series of problems and setbacks which at times seemed insurmountable.

To all these people and organisations, my sincere thanks.

Introduction

Over the past twenty years I have had the good fortune to travel widely, especially in the countries of South-East Asia, East Africa, and South America. During that time and in those areas I have seen how wildlife and wild places have been diminishing at a frightening rate as human populations have been expanding. The rain forests of Indonesia are disappearing so fast that it may not be long before the gentle orang utan is without a habitat in which it can survive. The safarilands of Africa, still among the world's great wonders, are under mounting threat from the tidal wave of humanity pressing against their boundaries. When one sees the desperate poverty of the Andean Indians it is hard to explain to them with conviction the underlying need for conserving the vicuña. In such places, as in many other parts of the world, the future of wildlife is truly in the balance.

When comparing our situation with that of less fortunate countries, can we in Britain really claim that our wildlife and wildlife habitats are threatened? I believe that unless present trends in land-use are checked, our wildlife is not just under threat, it is in grave danger, for we seem to be embarked on a headlong rush to transform the face of our countryside. If you go down to the woods today you may indeed get a surprise: there is a strong likelihood that the woods may not be there.

However, we British have forever been last-ditch defenders. Just when those of us concerned over wildlife conservation were beginning to despair, a law was passed, the Wildlife and Countryside Act, which went some way towards dealing with these problems. Some believe that it may prove to be only a transitional measure, but at least a start has been made. The purpose of this book is to bring attention to the Act by showing the reasons why it was necessary, outlining its main aims, and presenting a picture of the principle species of fauna and flora with which it is concerned.

The Act is not as comprehensive as one might have wished, nor is it very straightforward. Though it replaced some earlier wildlife legislation – the Protection of Birds Acts 1954–1967, and the Conservation of Wild Creatures and Wild Plants Act 1975 – it left several other Acts intact (with some amendments), among them the Badgers Act 1973, the Conservation of Seals Act 1970, and the Deer Act 1963.

Though reasonably satisfactory in dealing with the protection of species, the Act is not nearly decisive enough about habitat protection. Indeed, it may not comply with the intentions of the Berne Convention on the Conservation of European Wildlife and Natural Habitats, of which Britain is one of the signatories. There are other anomalies giving rise for concern, but they are beyond the scope of this book, which is of necessity selective.

Whereas the Act protects some 250 species, ranging from the barn owl to the lady's slipper, we have confined ourselves to 172 species, all chosen for carefully considered reasons. For example, of the 88 birds that are specially protected by the Act we have included 59 – the criteria being rarity, degree of threat, and the extent to which a bird is – or seems likely to become – a genuine British breeding species. Though some of the birds included are on the increase, they still remain scarce.

Others are excluded because they breed so rarely in Britain. It was difficult to draw the line between species which are irregular vagrants attempting to breed and those which also might be termed vagrants but which appear to be colonising. No doubt some ornithologists will question my choice, but I hope that it provides a useful pointer to the threats that our birdlife faces, as well as underlining some undoubted success stories.

With regard to other animals, we have included *all* the species listed in Schedule 5 of the Act – many of which now enjoy protection for the first time – but have omitted some others which are given only partial protection (under Schedule 6, for example). It may be thought that there was a case for including the badger, especially as there is evidence of an increase in the appalling practice of badger-digging. (Between 1974 and 1982 there were 146 convictions under the Badgers Act.) Perhaps we should also have included the pine marten, but by the same criteria that would have meant giving space to the polecat and the wild cat. All three are in fact increasing their range.

Though we have included *all* the plants which are now specially protected, regretfully we have had to omit many others – some of them equally rare and threatened – which are not listed in the Act.

In arriving at the list of 172 species I sought expert advice, but the final choice was my own. I therefore make no claim that this is a definitive inventory, but regard it more as a selective guide aimed at a general readership. The photographs speak for themselves, presenting a continuous spectacle of beauty and variety and contrast from one page to another. Who, having studied them, would want to see the last of the childling pink or the downy woundwort, the hen harrier or the wryneck, the mole cricket or the natterjack toad? Even the wonderfully descriptive common names are a time-honoured part of our natural heritage.

One or two other points need further explanation or comment. In the plant section, where the terms 'endangered', 'vulnerable', and 'rare' are used, I have followed the classification of Perring and Farrell in their *British Red Data Book 1: Vascular Plants*. Elsewhere, my use of these terms is based on other considerations. When describing locations I have often used the old county names, because most of the older distribution records refer to these areas, rather than the post-1974 counties. And I have tried to avoid revealing the precise locations of the rarest species of animals and plants in order to minimise possible threats from collectors.

We had great difficulty in finding suitable photographs of some of the rarer species, and in the case of the glutinous snail, the Essex emerald moth, and the reddish buff moth, we had to resort to museum specimens. If any reader should know of photographs of these species, we would be very grateful for information.

While researching the book I have learned a great deal, and much of it is disturbing. It may be an exaggeration to say, as Shakespeare once did of Scotland (in *Macbeth*), 'I think our country sinks beneath the yoke; it weeps, it bleeds; and each new day a gash is added to her wounds', but there is no doubt that the problem is a serious one.

A fundamental cause may be the vast disparity between the subsidies, grants, and other financial inducements available to encourage production on the land, compared with the sums available for protection of the countryside and its wildlife. Richard Body (Conservative MP for Holland-with-Boston and himself a farmer) has estimated that something like £3,000 million is spent each year in support of agriculture. By contrast, the budget of the Nature Conservancy Council is around £13 million.

An examination of the true costs of agriculture and of the EEC's mountains of surplus butter, wheat, and beef suggests that we are encouraging expensive and wasteful over-production. What is more, this ever-increasing production may not in the long run be sustainable.

There are two important steps which we could take. One would be to accept the proposed EEC Directive on Environmental Impact Assessments. This would enable us to obtain a much more balanced picture of the true costs and benefits of many schemes affecting the countryside. We might well conclude that they are not as necessary as those who plan them would have us believe. The other is to give serious thought to the introduction of statutory controls on land-use.

It has been calculated that three million people in Britain belong to conservation societies. Many millions more obviously believe that conservation is important. If enough of us want something to happen, it will happen. It won't be easy to change the course of our new agricultural (and forestry) revolution, but I am sure that it can be achieved. It is my hope that by revealing the dangers, this book will play a part in bringing about the necessary changes.

London, 1983

1 Mosaic of Change

This book is concerned with the threatened animals and plants of Britain, but before commenting on the reasons for their rarity and what can or should be done to ensure their protection it is important to give a general idea of how they and their different habitats evolved.

Many diverse factors have shaped Britain's landscape, some of them natural, some of them man-made. By far the most important natural factor was the effect of ice.

Over the past two million years several major glaciations, or Ice Ages, affected the British Isles. Some were extremely severe and extensive, covering most of the land with ice which was more than a mile thick in places. As the great ice masses advanced, they moulded hills and gouged out what are now lakes and river basins. A vast amount of water was locked up in the ice, so the sea level was several hundred feet lower than it is now.

The final Ice Age, which lasted for about 60,000 years, was less extensive than earlier ones, but nevertheless ice covered Scotland, Wales, most of Ireland, and parts of Northern England, the Midlands, and East Anglia. The ice-free region, which encompassed areas of Yorkshire and the Midlands and the whole of England south of a line joining the Severn and the Wash, was still fairly inhospitable – resembling the Arctic tundra of today – and the flora which grew there consisted of ground-covering plants such as mountain avens, mosses, sedges, and lichens. Among the fauna were reindeer, lemming, mammoth and woolly rhinoceros, and birds such as the ptarmigan and the dunlin. At this time Ireland was still joined to Britain, and Britain to the continent of Europe, so terrestrial creatures were free to wander wherever conditions were suitable.

This last glaciation came to an end between 10,000 and 12,000 years ago, and as the ice melted, plants and animals were able to spread northwards. First came birch, followed by pine and then by hazel.

With the continued improvement in the climate, the birch and pine – also other plants and associated fauna – moved farther northwards and were supplanted by elm and oak, which formed extensive forests of broad-leaved trees. When the climate became wetter, alder and lime made their appearance. (It is worth mentioning that because they have never been cultivated, some of the high mountain grasslands of the north, and areas such as Upper Teesdale, probably still contain the same kind of flora and fauna as they did at the end of the Ice Ages.)

As the ice melted, so the sea level began to rise, and eventually – between 8,000 and 7,000 years ago – Britain was separated from the Continent. From that time onwards terrestrial animals could no longer freely migrate.

Ireland was separated from Britain during an earlier period: the channel between Scotland and Ireland is deeper than the English Channel (about 200 feet compared with 60 feet), and this separation by the sea determined the numbers of amphibians, reptiles and mammals in the two islands. Migration was no longer possible for land animals nor for freshwater fishes (most of which probably arrived when the Thames and other eastern rivers were still tributaries of the Rhine), and the spread of plants was restricted. However, this did not apply to birds and other flying animals such as bats and insects. Even those with poor powers of flight could easily have been blown across on a favourable wind, or carried by stronger fliers. Seeds and spores of plants can also be carried by the wind, and it is well established that birds are a major agent in the dispersal of seeds, either in their stomachs or adhering to their legs and feathers.

It is interesting to speculate how our fauna and flora might have developed if the land bridge with Europe had not been severed. There would certainly be more species, though some would probably be restricted to the warmer regions of the South-East. Taking just one group, there are only 41 native land mammals in Great Britain, compared with 167 in Western Europe. Undoubtedly others could exist here, too. The fact that this country offers suitable conditions for species other than those that managed to get across in time is clear from the number that have subsequently been introduced, either accidentally or deliberately, and are now thriving.

= ALIEN SPE.

Comparatively few species have become extinct since Britain became an island. Among the mammals we have lost are the aurochs, lynx, wolf, brown bear, wild boar, and beaver. The wall lizard, the green lizard and the agile frog may also have colonised Britain for a few thousand years, until a later climate deterioration, combined with habitat alteration by early man, caused them to disappear.

After the effect of glaciation, the next most important natural influence on our landscape has been geological. Britain is composed of a great variety of rocks and soils – perhaps greater than that of any other similar-sized area of the world. The most ancient rocks are in the North-West of Scotland and the youngest are in South-East England. Older mountain rocks are harder in substance and less prone to erosion, while younger rocks tend to be softer and to erode more readily, forming flatter landscapes and adding more of their nutrients to the soil. By determining the topography and the nature of the soil, the basic geographical structure of the land directly influences the habitats and evolution of wildlife.

A third fundamental influence on wildlife and its habitats is climate. The British Isles are located quite far to the north, roughly at the same latitude as Labrador, with Glasgow more or less on the same level as Moscow, but our climate, especially in the west, is greatly modified by the warm waters of the Gulf Stream. The west of Britain is also fairly wet, because of the moisture carried by winds off the North Atlantic. The east is drier, as by the time that the westerly winds arrive they have deposited most of their rain. Eastern Britain is affected, too, by its proximity to Europe, and is colder in winter and warmer in the summer than the more equable west.

Because Britain spans some nine degrees of latitude from north to south, Scotland is cooler than southern England – though it has longer days in summer, which means a longer growing season. Since temperatures decrease considerably with altitude, high mountains are colder than the lowlands. Thus the growing season at 2,000 feet may be effectively half that at sea level. Higher ground is also inclined to be wetter, because air cools as it rises and loses its capacity to hold water, which it deposits in the form of rain.

Before concluding this summary of the influence of natural factors on our wildlife and its wonderfully diverse habitats it is worth pointing out that the ice has not necessarily retreated forever. We may now be experiencing merely a temperate interlude in the long succession of Ice Ages. Scientists predict that in 1,000 years' time our planet may shift its orbit very slightly, precipitating another severe glaciation which could be more extreme than the last one. Such considerations are rather beyond the scope of this book – but it seems to me that if there are still animals and plants and human beings on the earth in a thousand years' time it will only be because man has managed to solve a great number of serious environmental problems. If science continues to advance as it has done in the past hundred years it is likely that some way will be found to prevent most of the Northern Hemisphere from being covered with ice. Meanwhile there are more immediate problems to concern us.

Whereas ice was the main natural factor in determining the broad pattern of our landscape and wildlife, the influence of man has gradually increased, and for the last 5,000 years has been predominant.

The very early human inhabitants of Britain had little effect on their environment. The palaeolithic and later the mesolithic peoples were really just another element in the fauna of these islands. Subsisting by hunting and plant gathering, they may have been responsible to a certain degree for bringing about the extinction of some large animals such as the mammoth and the wild horse. But in general they made no serious impact on the wildlife. However, with the arrival of the neolithic people about 3,000 BC, a watershed was reached.

Neolithic men were farmers who grew crops and understood animal husbandry. Their way of life necessitated the clearance of forest, and it was they who first began the long process during which Britain's countryside was transformed from a wholly natural environment to an essentially man-made one. They stripped the ancient forests – the 'wildwood' – for fuel, for building materials, and particularly to create clearings where they could graze their animals and plant their crops. They tended to select drier places and more exposed regions where the trees were less dense and easier to fell with their primitive tools. So it was the uplands that were first transformed. As these areas were cleared, wild flowers – which had previously been unable to flourish under the trees – began to take root, and in many places the uplands gradually became covered in blanket bog.

After the introduction of metals to Britain around 2,000 BC, the process of clearance was speeded up and extended. With the arrival of the Celts and their more sophisticated agricultural techniques, around 500 BC, the process was further increased. By the time that the Romans came to Britain there was fairly extensive cultivation on lighter soils and on higher ground, but most of the English lowlands were still covered mainly with oak forests through which roamed wolves, bears, and large herds of deer. These regions were, as a whole, uninhabited.

Oak forests also clothed the sides of valleys in hill and mountain regions of the west and north, while on the poor and sandy soils there were woods of pine and birch. Though more land was cleared in Roman times, the essential character of the country's vegetation was virtually unchanged. During this period, however, there was a great increase in sheep grazing on the uplands; previously the important domestic animals had been cattle and pigs, which were principally woodland creatures.

The next major event in the changing of Britain's landscape was the coming of the Saxons in the fifth century. They were lowland cultivators and began to clear the forests from valleys and low-lying plains. As they annihilated the Celts or forced them westwards, cultivation of the hills and plateaux more or less came to an end, though in some areas sheep were still grazed. It was thus the Saxons who converted England from a mainly forest-covered land to one that was largely agricultural.

With the coming of the Normans in the eleventh century there was a temporary pause in the process of landscape transformation. At first the Normans laid waste large parts of the country to demonstrate their strength. Crops were destroyed, and fields were probably taken over by wild vegetation before they were later adopted once more for agriculture. As the Normans were devoted to hunting, they established a number of Royal Forests (which were not necessarily tree-covered). Cultivation in the forests was discouraged, at least on any but a small scale. It has been suggested that during these times as much as a third of England came under Forest Law.

Certainly the Norman period brought a check in the conversion of wild countryside to agricultural land, but at the end of the twelfth century the process had started again, and the expansion of crop-raising and animal-grazing was to continue throughout the Middle Ages.

A. G. Tansley has described one aspect of the process: 'Side by side with the clearance of forest land for tillage went the grazing of cattle, as well as pigs, in the forest itself. It is believed that the feeding of swine in oak or beech forests actually assisted regeneration of woodland through the pigs stamping a certain proportion of acorns or beechnuts into the soil, where they are more likely to germinate successfully than when they lie on the surface. Also, the destruction by the pigs of small vermin such as slugs, snails, mice, and voles – which today make regeneration impossible by destroying the nuts and seedling trees – would work in the same direction. But the extensive pasturing of *cattle* in the forest always leads to the disappearance of the woodland plants, consolidation of the soil by trampling, and the introduction of grass vegetation – conditions which make the germination and establishment of tree seedlings more difficult, apart from their destruction by browsing, and thus lead to the disappearance of the forests as old trees die.'

So the forest was inexorably cleared, degenerating into rough grassland and heathland, interspersed with large thorny shrubs such as hawthorn, blackthorn, and gorse which were able to withstand grazing by animals. During the Middle Ages, farming for profit mostly replaced subsistence farming, and at various times sizeable amounts of corn, wool and cloth were exported.

The proportion of land devoted to either arable farming or pasture depended on fluctuations in the price of different products – a situation that is not unfamiliar today. In mediaeval times the textile industry was prosperous, and at various periods huge flocks of sheep were maintained: it has been estimated that around the year 1350 there were some eight million sheep in England, that is four times as many sheep as people. The amount of grassland increased enormously, and continued to increase for centuries. By the start of the Second World War some fifty per cent of the land area of England and Wales was under 'permanent' grass.

Though Britain's native forest or woodland had been declining at the hand of man for some thousands of years, the pace quickened considerably after the disafforestation of the Norman Royal Forests. By the fourteenth century, timber was already being imported, especially into Eastern England; by the sixteenth century, major shortages were felt; and by the seventeenth, the reserves of native forest were exhausted. In 1685 foreign timber had to be imported to build ships for the Royal Navy, as the supply of suitable oak planks was no longer adequate. The final death-knell of the English forests came with the demand for fuel by the iron-smelting and glass-making industries in the sixteenth and seventeenth centuries – although some woodland, which might otherwise have been converted into farmland, was preserved by these industries in the form of coppice.

'Coppicing' involves cutting down a young tree or shrub to just above ground level at regular intervals (about eight years for hazel). This produces a fine crop of slender saplings growing from the stump, which in the past were used for a wide variety of purposes. Though hazel was particularly popular for coppicing, other trees such as ash, sweet chestnut, and hornbeam were similarly treated. In a typical coppice, some oak trees were generally allowed to grow to full size, at a density of perhaps twelve to the acre. Not being very close together, the oaks grew strong, spreading branches that provided the curved timber needed for ship-building. This kind of coppice was called 'coppice-with-standards'.

One advantage of oak-hazel coppices, compared with a dense oak forest, is that it allows in more light. Though this brings about a more vigorous growth of the shrub layer, it also encourages the field layer of wild flowers. The familiar English woodland is mainly this type of coppice-with-standards (though coppicing hardly takes place any more) with its carpets of spring flowers.

Though in southern Scotland the forests were disappearing about a hundred years before those of England, in the Highlands it was a different story. In the valleys and glens there was still a fair amount of virgin forest – oak at lower altitudes and pine or birch on poorer soils and higher up. However, around the beginning of the seventeenth century, exploitation began in earnest, especially for charcoal, which was needed in iron smelting. The forest that was not stripped for this purpose was cleared later in the eighteenth and nineteenth centuries, as sheep farming expanded in the Highlands.

If proof should be needed of the nature of forest land and of the way in which it once dominated our countryside, reference can be made to a revealing experiment which began in Hertfordshire in 1882. A half-acre plot in a wheat field at Rothamsted Experimental Station was fenced in to see what would happen. As Ralph Whitlock explains (1979): 'At the end of four years, competition by weeds had eliminated all but a few stunted wheat plants. Gradually the arable weeds were smothered by brambles and bushes, and these in their turn had to yield place to trees. Now the half acre is a dense wood of trees 60 to 70 feet tall, the chief species of which are hawthorn, oak, ash, and sycamore. In parts the tree-cover is so dense that only trailing ivy will grow beneath it; elsewhere there is a thick growth of bramble and dog's mercury. The natural vegetation of the heavy soil at Rothamsted, typical of the Midlands, is thus clearly demonstrated.'

As well as forest and woodland, several other important features of our landscape have been similarly reshaped by the hand of man. For example, fens and marshes, which once covered large areas of lowland Britain, were gradually drained, first in Roman times for military purposes, and later to create agricultural land and to provide sea defences. The Norfolk and Suffolk Broads were formed by the massive extraction of peat during mediaeval times. In the seventeenth century considerable areas of wetland were drained. This pressure to transform such 'useless' land still continues today.

Hedgerows are an intrinsic feature of the British countryside but, like much else that we treasure, they are man-made. 'Without hedges, England would not be England,' wrote Richard Jeffries in 1884. Since Saxon times, hedges have been used to enclose fields and to define the boundaries of manors and parishes. Some of the earliest hedges may be remnants of the original forest formed when settlers first cleared patches of land. Many hedges were planted following the Enclosure Acts of the eighteenth and nineteenth centuries, when millions of acres of wasteland, open fields, and common pasture were enclosed.

It is a common misconception that our countrywide network of hedges dates largely from the enclosures, and that they are therefore no more than 200 years old. Oliver Rackham, however, has estimated that perhaps half our hedges date from between the Bronze Age and the seventeenth century. These older hedges tend to meander through the countryside following natural features such as valley bottoms, and are therefore more in harmony with the landscape than more recent ones which were laid out in geometrical patterns. Max Hooper has shown that in general terms a hedge gains one new species of tree or shrub with every century, so that a hedgerow with ten or more species of woody plant in a thirty-yard stretch may date from Saxon times.

Hedges provide extremely rich wildlife habitats, and are increasingly important nowadays as many other habitats disappear. They harbour nearly a thousand native British plants. Most birds resident in woodland will also breed in hedges, which are a kind of woodland in miniature (more accurately, like a coppice-with-standards); and many other birds feed in them. Nearly half our native British mammals can be found in hedges. More than twenty species of butterfly breed in them, while a large number of useful insects inhabit hedges, including those that pollinate crops, and others that are predators or parasites on crop pests.

Just as so-called 'natural' features such as hedges, downland, and heathland provide a wealth of habitats, so other more obviously man-made features harbour a variety of wildlife. Motorway verges and central reservations seem attractive to creatures such as the field vole, which in turn attract kestrels, as anyone who often drives on motorways will know. Motorway edges also provide good plant habitats. In 1959 the verges of the M1 were sown with only four species of grass but a survey revealed that by the early 1970s some 400 plant species were growing between Hendon and Leeds. Airports, railways, sewage farms, refuse tips, reservoirs, quarries, churchyards and cemeteries – all have their distinctive fauna and flora.

Our towns and cities, too, provide a home for a surprisingly wide variety of animals and plants. The urban fox is now a well-known phenomenon, and many other animals find that a built up environment offers suitable accommodation and food. In the space of a few days in London I have seen kestrels in Chelsea, great crested newts in Bromley, orchids in Barking, herons in Hackney, and a solitary common broomrape lurking at the edge of a colossal rubbish dump near King's Cross Station. The small gardens of our urban areas represent a significant network of tiny nature reserves, while city parks are potentially even more important: if only local authorities could be persuaded to moderate their desire to tidy up by constantly mowing the grass. Of course, gardens and parkland in suburbia and the countryside are even more important for wildlife.

Whether man-made or natural, Britain has a diversity of wildlife habitats which probably surpasses that of any country of comparable size in the world. To ignore the consequences of converting this richly varied landscape into monotonous stretches of cropland and comparatively lifeless tracts of conifer is short-sighted in the extreme. Though some of us may be unaware of it, we are all affected by our environment, and it makes perfect sense that we should seek to preserve the features which give the British landscape its unique quality – copses and spinneys, ancient hedgerows, streams and rivers, fens and marshes, heaths and downs, mountain and moorland – and with them the plants and animals to which they in turn give life.

2 The Price of Progress

Individual species of animals and plants do not necessarily have everlasting life. Evolutionists know that some will respond to changes in their environment by evolving into other species, while some less fortunate ones, lacking such evolutionary adaptability, will lose out to 'fitter' species and will become extinct. It has been estimated that no more than one-tenth of all the species of life forms that have inhabited the earth remain with us. This means that ninety per cent have vanished for all time.

The process of gradual change, the replacement of one life form by another, still continues in the natural world. No doubt it is happening among the myriad insect populations deep in the remaining South American forests, among little-known creatures in the oceans, and also among the plants. But there is now a new element in the evolutionary equation: the effect of man's presence as an instrument of change. Whether we call this element unnatural or artificial is unimportant. What is important is that we recognise that human activities exert a greater pressure on animals and plants than their inherited survival mechanisms can cope with. Some species can profit by or at least resist this pressure. Malaria-carrying mosquitoes have proved all too able to evolve strains resistant to DDT. In Britain the rabbit has managed to survive in spite of myxomatosis. Some insects have increased to pest proportions because we have removed their natural predators. Yet other organisms have found the new environmental conditions created by man much to their liking: the house sparrow is a good example, as is the starling (though in its case climatic improvement may have been the dominant influence). In urban areas of North America, European species such as the sparrow, starling and feral pigeon have become ubiquitous, rather than the native American species: the European birds have a much longer history of living with humans and therefore a greater ability to benefit from the human environment.

As well as man's influence, however, natural factors such as climate are still important. It is more likely that reindeer and lemmings disappeared from Britain when the ice retreated simply because it became too warm for them, rather than because they were exterminated by man. It is a biogeographical fact that the farther towards the poles you go the fewer species you will find, so it is not surprising that there are not nearly as many animal and plant species in Britain as there are nearer to the equator. Similarly, there is not such a rich variety in the far north of Scotland as in the southern counties of England.

A number of our animals and plants are at the edge of their natural range in this country, and as some species are adapted to life in more northerly regions, when they occur in Scotland they are at the southern edge of their range. Mostly, however, our rarer species are inclined to be southern forms finding a foothold in the southern part of the country.

The smallest climatic change can therefore affect our native fauna and flora. For example, during very hot, dry summers, some reptiles and amphibians seek refuge in the comparatively cool and moist conditions of woodlands. If there were no woodlands, they would probably suffer greater population losses.

Insects are especially susceptible to unsuitable climatic conditions because, in most cases, in order to survive, they have to breed every year, and they need suitable conditions at each stage of their life cycles. When numbers are already low, bad weather can be critical. The unfortunate large blue butterfly, already suffering from a reduction in suitable habitat, was hit by unfavourable weather conditions in the mid-seventies, and in 1979 it became extinct.

The effects of climate are also particularly noticeable among our breeding birds. Climatic changes are thought to be responsible for the decline of such species as the cirl bunting and the roseate tern, while the Dartford warbler is known to be affected by hard winters. The wryneck has disappeared and the red-backed shrike seems on the point of disappearing from southern Britain almost certainly because of climatic changes – but in these two cases there is compensation, in the apparent colonisation of Scotland by birds of the same species, originating from Scandinavia.

All animals suffer during spells of unsuitable weather. In February 1983 huge numbers of dead and dying seabirds – mainly razorbills, guillemots, and puffins – were washed ashore along the east coast of Britain from Edinburgh to Kent. Young as well as adult birds were affected, and the British Trust for Ornithology concluded that the massive mortality (well over 13,000 birds) was caused by a spell of stormy weather in the North Sea. As such climatic events are part of nature's pattern, they should not be cause for too much concern – that is, in relation to species which are widespread and numerous and which are not unduly affected by other adverse circumstances such as loss of habitat. Natural catastrophes have a much greater significance when a species is already under pressure for some other reason.

Since man first began to exert his influence on the environment, the range of threats to wildlife has multiplied, and even a cursory glance through the International Union for Conservation of Nature's *Red Data Books* (listing internationally threatened species) reveals numerous examples of animals that have become scarce through direct human persecution. Sometimes the reason is that the animals are large and considered dangerous to man. Others are killed for their valuable skins, horns, teeth, shells, feathers, or even as souvenirs. Some are hunted for sport, others to bring back live as pets or for exhibition in zoos. Many are killed for food.

British fauna has not been as subject to this kind of direct persecution as that of other countries. In the past, it is true, we lost a few large mammals and birds, but as the human population expanded and the available habitat declined in our small land this was probably inevitable. Wolves and bears could hardly co-exist with 56 million people in about the same number of acres. Nevertheless, some British species have suffered at man's hand, especially from hunting (both for food and sport), and because they were competing for the same prey.

Deer, of course, have been hunted from time immemorial. The roe deer vanished from England – except in the extreme north – but was subsequently reintroduced (it never became extinct in Scotland). Neither red nor roe nor any introduced deer species are today in any danger; indeed, they can often cause quite a lot of damage and have to be controlled.

Three animals whose numbers were once greatly reduced by hunting are the pine marten and wild cat (hunted for sport and as vermin), and polecat (vermin). However, the numbers of all three have increased and they no longer appear to be threatened.

Snakes invariably suffer from an inherent human anathema towards them. In fact only one of our three snakes, the adder, is poisonous. Very few people die from adder bites: only ten fatalities have been recorded in the past century, and just two since 1950. Even dogs that are bitten on the nose or throat seldom die. Yet adders are mercilessly killed, as are the harmless grass snake and the rare and innocuous smooth snake. Of these three reptiles only the smooth snake is fully protected, and in this respect Britain is now out of step with much of Europe – especially Northern and Eastern Europe, where the killing of snakes, except perhaps the most poisonous species, is illegal.

The grey seal and the far less numerous common seal, regarded by fishermen as pests, were regularly hunted in the past. Grey seal numbers once dropped so low that in 1914 the species came under legal protection. Now both species are protected during their breeding seasons. In recent years much attention has been focussed on the grey seal because of culling in Orkney. This has aroused the anger of conservationists and animal welfare organisations who believe that not enough is known about the biology of the grey seal and who therefore question the accusation that it is a serious threat to fisheries. From recent evidence it would now seem that it is not a particularly serious pest, though it is undoubtedly responsible for occasionally damaging salmon nets. If seal numbers were substantially reduced, fish yields might increase minimally, but not greatly. Neither would the value of the fish catch (which is what most concerns fishermen) necessarily improve very much, for with some fish species price is determined by quantity. The more fish that are landed, the lower the price.

Little might be gained from resuming the seal cull – and much lost. The British grey seal population is over 80,000, which represents over two-thirds of the total world population.

The brown hare has long been hunted, by shooting, coursing, and beagling. None of these activities seems to have had any great effect on hare numbers, yet hares are steadily declining. A recent study by Dr Richard Barnes and Dr Stephen Tapper showed that the number of hares killed in a given area in 1980 was only half the 1965 figure. Unfavourable weather and depredation by foxes may have been partly responsible (hares probably constitute up to only a quarter of a rural fox's diet, but foxes have increased three-fold in the last two decades).

According to the two scientists, a more significant reason for the hare's decline is the change in farming practices. Hares are very selective feeders, visiting particular crops only for short periods; one hare may travel over an area as large as 125 acres every year in search of a variety of crops. Ideally, it chooses a site where it has easy access to several fields where different crops are grown. Unfortunately, however, the modern tendency towards very large fields under monoculture precludes the required variety. Under such circumstances the hares enlarge their range, but their population density drops by as much as two-thirds. They may also be affected by the herbicide paraquat, which in the autumn is often applied to weeds growing in stubble before it is burned, and which the animals absorb by licking their fur.

Our fifteen British bats suffer from an even larger number of hazards than the hare. For some species, information is somewhat sketchy but enough is known to prove that most bat numbers have declined at a frightening rate over the past century. For example, while numbers of the greater horseshoe bat have diminished by 95 per cent in a hundred years, the more common species decreased by 50 per cent in only two years. The causes include bad weather at critical periods in their life cycle, pollution, and loss of feeding habitat, food, and roosting sites.

Bats once frequented woodland and river valleys, and roosted in hollow trees and caves. Nowadays old trees with holes (which also harbour a number of other creatures) are often regarded as dangerous and are felled, while riverside trees are removed during canalisation projects. As tree cover has decreased, bats have adapted to living in old buildings, but such places are not necessarily secure for long – because access holes such as ventilators may be blocked, cavity walls filled for insulation, and roofs retiled and lined with under-felt.

An even greater threat to bat colonies is timber treatment. Each year more than 100,000 buildings are impregnated with chemicals to destroy woodworm. The compounds used are lethal to bats and are extremely persistent, so that even if bats are not present during treatment, when they return to roost they can be poisoned by inhaling the vapour or by contact with the treated surfaces.

Bats still frequent caves, but in this country such habitats are found only in a few localities. Some colonies have taken to roosting in mines and old railway tunnels, but in the past thirty years many of these have been filled in by rubbish-tipping or for safety reasons. Bats are also quite prone to disturbance by pot-holers and archaeologists, and in some cases colonies of hibernating bats have been destroyed by vandals.

As if all this were not enough, the number and variety of night-flying insects has been reduced by habitat changes, including the disappearance of woodlands and hedges. Also, the decline in hay-making has resulted in fewer insects reaching maturity, which means, for instance, that the larger bats cannot find enough cockchafer beetles on which to feed when they emerge from hibernation – the time at which they need them most.

As a group, bats must be among the most threatened of Britain's wild animals. Though they are afforded greater protection than other fauna, it remains to be seen whether legal sanctions will be enough to save them from eventful extinction.

If we should ever wonder what our forefathers enjoyed eating we may find at least one clue in the familiar nursery rhyme about 'Four and twenty blackbirds, baked in a pie'. In days gone by a wide variety of birds were hunted and eaten, many of them species that we in Britain would not think of eating today. (Unhappily for migratory species, attitudes in some European and Mediterranean countries are not so enlightened.) The coronation banquet of King Henry VI is said to have featured lark, swan, heron, crane, bittern, plover, and curlew. Other species that were once considered good to eat included dotterel, ruff, and godwit.

Nowadays, only a few wild birds are in any danger of being hunted for the pot, though in some backwaters old ideas linger on. In 1983 (quite a while after the Wildlife and Countryside Act came into force) I met a member of the British Field Sports Society who extolled the merits of roast greenshank. He did not seem disturbed at the prospect of a £1,000 fine.

During the last century, and earlier in this one, too, birds of prey were ruthlessly persecuted, as they were considered unacceptable intruders on sporting estates. First, the keepers shot and trapped them. Then, as they became rarer, the collectors stepped in to secure specimens of eggs or skins. The attentions of collectors affected many other birds, but birds of prey were hard hit, especially by game keepers. Ospreys, for example, were lured by gin traps baited with trout just below the surface of the water. Though the raptors have recovered from those bad times, they still face a greater variety of problems than other birds. Richard Porter and Michael Everett of the Royal Society for the Protection of Birds summarise the position as follows:

Habitat destruction, such as afforestation of upland moorland, can deprive hen harriers and merlins of breeding areas. As many birds of prey are very wide-

19

ranging, the setting up of nature reserves is only a partial solution.

Pollution by agricultural pesticides. Since they are at the end of a food chain, birds of prey can accumulate high levels of toxic chemicals from their prey, causing a reduction in breeding or even death. During the 1950s and 1960s the populations of several species, especially peregrines and sparrowhawks, diminished alarmingly. Since the introduction of voluntary bans on the use of the more persistent pesticides, populations have recovered. However, in some parts of the country some species are still accumulating unacceptable levels of certain chemicals.

Poisoning. Many raptors die as a result of eating poisoned bait, the use of which is illegal. In 1982 the RSPB learned of nearly 60 cases of deliberate poisoning, many involving birds of prey including white-tailed and golden eagles, buzzards, and red kite. According to reports received by government organisations, in 1982 there were probably over 100 cases of deliberate poisoning.

Persecution. In some areas, especially those managed for sporting interests, birds of prey can be particularly unpopular. In 1982, 36 reports were received of shooting and destruction, in addition to deliberate poisoning. Hen harriers and goshawks are considered the Number One Enemy by keepers.

Egg stealing. Peregrines, red kites, and golden eagles are still sought after by unscrupulous collectors. Of 72 egg-collecting incidents reported to the RSPB in 1983, by far the greatest number applied to raptors.

Illegal taking of birds of prey. The peregrine, goshawk, merlin, and even the common kestrel, are the main targets, with 127 reports in 1982 involving illegal taking, possession, or sale.

The RSPB is concerned about the persistent trade in illegally taken birds of prey, many of which are exported for high prices. Before the 1983 breeding season had ended, the Society knew of more than 70 peregrine eyries that had been robbed. With an average of four eggs per nest, this could have meant 280 peregrines, taken either as eggs to be hatched in incubators or as young birds which are placed in aviaries to support fraudulent claims of captive breeding. At about the same time, 253 peregrine eggs were registered as having been laid in captivity; and 250 to 300 fully-grown peregrines had also been registered. (Registration and ringing of captive birds of prey is now compulsory under the Wildlife and Countryside Act.) In the summer of 1983 the Department of the Environment issued a general licence permitting anyone to sell peregrines, goshawks, merlins, and golden eagles that had been registered, close-ringed, and bred in captivity. To quote Ian Prestt, Director of the RSPB: 'With the high level of nest thefts, and the acknowledged difficulty of breeding peregrines in captivity, many sales must be regarded with suspicion.'

Birds' eggs are not the only items which attract collectors. Butterflies and moths are irresistible, as are some other invertebrates. As a young man, Charles Darwin was an avid collector and a story is told that when out collecting beetles at Cambridge he was carrying a rare species in each hand, when he saw a third. He could not bear to let it go, so he put one of the two that he was holding into his mouth. 'Alas it ejected some intensely acrid fluid, which burnt my tongue so that I was forced to spit the beetle out, which was lost, as well as the third one.'

Huge numbers of insects and birds' eggs were collected in Victorian times: indeed the New Forest burnet moth seems to have been exterminated from its original habitat by professional collectors. Though collecting on a commercial scale has ceased, there are still people who succumb to temptation. During my researches I was dismayed to find one eminent authority writing of a particularly rare species that 'so gorgeous is the [———] that it is every collector's dream to find one'.

The uprooting of plants is now illegal, except on private property, but it still continues: particularly in the case of the rarer flora such as alpines, and the more showy species such as orchids. The lady's slipper has been reduced to a single plant almost certainly because of collecting, and some other orchids still suffer depredation. Although conservation-minded botanists try to keep secret the location of rare species, collectors seem to have an uncanny knack of tracking them down. During the flowering season certain orchids now have to be guarded around the clock by volunteer wardens aided by trip-wire alarms. Even these precautions are not always successful.

While collecting is a major threat to some rare plants, others are affected by the trampling feet of hikers, climbers, and casual visitors. At risk from this danger are plant species on the sea coast and in mountain areas. Plants in Snowdonia are particularly vulnerable. Sometimes even the most well-intentioned person can unwittingly cause damage. On one occasion, for example, a keen photographer was observed taking a picture of a rare plant with a close-up lens . . . and as he did so he destroyed two other plants of the same species by lying on them.

In their extremely important *Vascular Plants* (British Red Data Books: 1), Franklin Perring and Lynne Farrell describe 317 rare or threatened flowering plants and ferns in Britain. Of these 19 are now actually extinct – though this is an encouragingly low figure, since it represents the extinctions noted since recording began in the seventeenth century. However, many of the others are declining, and a total of 51 plants are considered endangered. Another 93 are vulnerable, and 154 are rare.

Listing these species under their different habitats Perring and Farrell show that the greatest number (38) of endangered and vulnerable species are plants of lowland pasture, open grassland, and other natural open habitats. The next most endangered group are the plants of wetland habitats (23), followed by the plants of woodland, scrub and hedge (20). Next come arable weeds with 17 species, followed by plants of man-made habitats, roadsides, and quarries (13).

Though 144 species on the list are classified as endangered or vulnerable, only 61 species are included in the Wildlife and Countryside Act. There are various reasons for this – one of them being that to some extent inclusion in the Act can serve to draw collectors' attention to a particular species.

A vulnerable plant not listed in the Act is the cut-leaved germander (*Teucrium botrys*). Among its past known localities was a site in Surrey that became a nudist colony 'where no reputable botanist has seen it recently'. It is not clear whether botanists who may have been to the nudist colony are considered disreputable, or whether reputable botanists have not been able to pluck up courage to go there and search for the germander.

Although roadside verges and motorway central reservations are known to be refuges for various kinds of wildlife – a kind of linear nature reserve – they can also be very destructive. Thousands of animals are killed when crossing roads – for example toads, en route to their breeding ponds, and badgers and hedgehogs. Though there is some evidence that many creatures are learning to be cautious about crossing roads, this does not yet seem to apply to toads.

Another species that is suffering is the barn owl, already under pressure from other dangers. Apparently the owls are attracted to the motorways by the large populations of small mammals that are also prey for kestrels in the daytime. The owls hunt by flying low over the ground and are often killed when they collide with cars and other vehicles. A recent survey carried out for the Hawk Trust suggests that this may be a major reason for the decline of the barn owl, as its numbers have diminished even in counties such as Devon and Hertfordshire where the other hazards which it faces are less severe.

Road construction can be equally damaging, just by swallowing up land. Between 1968 and 1978 the Department of Transport built 938 miles of motorway – which may have accounted for 40,000 acres of countryside. Having researched current road building plans, Friends of the Earth reveal that many major projects cut through Sites of Special Scientific Interest (see beginning of Chapter 3) up and down the country. These include unspoiled chalk downland near Winchester (M3); heathland in Devon (North Devon Link Road); the only wet bog in rural Warwickshire (approach to M6 interchange); Brettenham Heath National Nature Reserve in Norfolk (widening of A11); ancient woodland near Oxted, Surrey (M25); Stoke Ferry, Norfolk (widening and drainage of A47); and the largest remaining example of alder carr in Northamptonshire (A43).

Many of us are ambivalent about road construction. I know that I personally am disturbed, if not outraged, when I see or hear of large expanses of countryside disappearing under the road-builders' bulldozers. Yet when I am driving I appreciate the convenience of motorways. The M40 provides a conveniently fast way of getting from London to Oxford, but it slices right through the middle of Aston Rowant, one of our smaller but most valuable National Nature Reserves which safeguards unimproved chalk grassland and mature woodland: habitats rich in native species of animals and plants.

A motorway that carves up a number of important natural sites is the M25, eventually due to encircle London. Ironically, while nature has had to take second place to the new road, the cricket ground of a small club called the Epping Foresters has come through unscathed. The road was scheduled to cut through the ground, but the Department of Transport was persuaded to build a 300-yard tunnel underneath it – at a cost of £12 million. The Transport Minister at the time, Norman Fowler, described this decision as 'a triumph for conservation and common sense'. In nature conservation terms, that comment and the thinking behind it can only be described as a black joke. No one begrudges the cricketers their field, but it would be more impressive if future generations of nature-lovers were offered similar opportunities to enjoy what *they* treasure – in the form of the precious natural sites that the M25 is likely to destroy.

So far in this review of the various threats to our wildlife I have referred to several serious problems affecting our flora, fauna, and wild places, but they are of minor significance when compared with the massive changes in land-use brought about by the demands of modern agriculture and forestry. These two industries are literally changing the face of Britain.

As Richard Mabey has pointed out in his book *The Common Ground,* it is not surprising, in view of this country's original forest cover and the variety of different woodland types – and thus the choice of habitats – that many of our animals and plants are adapted to woodland conditions. 'Two-thirds of our breeding land-birds, more than half our butterflies and moths, and one-sixth of our flowering plants are exclusively or chiefly dependent on woodlands. If we were to add those more adaptable species that occur in other habitats as well, and those that use woods casually from time to time, it would be possible to find, somewhere in the complex of woodland habitats, virtually the entire range of our flora and fauna.'

Most lowland deciduous woodland is best described as 'semi-natural', as for centuries it has been managed either as coppice or as wood pasture. Coppice provided a renewable supply of wood for fuel, timber for building, and materials for making fencing, hurdles, baskets, handles, and other implements. Wood pasture consisted of more open woodland with large trees from which the branches were periodically cut, and where deer, cattle, and horses grazed. Increasingly over the last century these traditional uses have declined, with foresters concentrating principally on plantations. And today plantations are generally of conifers, not broadleaved trees.

There are still about 740,000 acres of broadleaved woodland, and this is being destroyed in two ways: by felling for conversion to farmland – which in the short term is more profitable for the owner – and for conversion to conifers, which are rather less profitable but of more commercial value than the original woodland. In addition, large areas of other land, mainly moorland in Northern England, Wales and Scotland is being converted to vast conifer plantations, especially by the Forestry Commission.

As conifers grow more quickly than broadleaved trees they produce a quicker financial return. Also, for the private landowner there are very real tax advantages in growing them. But what wildlife can we expect to see in a conifer plantation? In the early stages, a number of species can be supported, including birds such as nightingales, nightjars, and hen harriers. But as the trees mature, the plantations become dark, silent places where few plants (other than the trees themselves) can grow, and few birds, mammals and reptiles can survive. Some of the tits may flourish, as may the newly colonising firecrest, but these are a poor substitute for the rich variety found in an old broadleaved wood. One influencing factor in this somewhat barren scene is the lack of insects. Fir trees can support a bare 16 insect species, while our native oak is associated with 284 different insects which either feed directly on it or prey on others that obtain their food from it.

It would appear that the most suitable trees for insects are our 'native' trees – those that arrived here naturally after the Ice Age – and have had a long period of time in which insects and other animals have been able to adapt to them. The native Scots pine, which deserves to be cherished in its own northern environment, plays host to 91 insects.

As well as providing only poor sustenance for wildlife, conifer plantations suffer from the fact that all the trees are of the same age and therefore do not offer the variety of habitats that occur in natural woodlands.

Woods and forests now cover about nine per cent of Britain's land area, but farmers are far bigger landowners, with agricultural holdings representing around 80 per cent of the total acreage. By no means all of this land consists of fields planted with crops. Much of it is rough grazing, and in between and fringing many of the fields are copses, shelterbelts, hedges, ponds, rivers, and bogs. One way and another, farmland provides food, shelter, and living space for most of our native wildlife.

Since the Second World War, productivity in the farming industry has increased tremendously. About 250 years ago half the nation's workforce was employed on the land. The current figure is around two per cent: one man now produces enough food to support 42 people. In the past thirty years wheat-yields per acre have more or less doubled, while barley-yields have increased by more than 60 per cent. Cows produce 48 per cent more milk and chickens 52 per cent more eggs. At the same time some 50,000 acres of good quality farmland have been lost every year.

This tremendous increase in agricultural production had been brought about at a price. And that price is quantified in two parts: one by very considerable and continuous injections of money, the other involving steady conversion of rough grazing to arable land suitable for growing wheat, barley, and other crops.

But in this book we are concerned not so much with the finances of the farming revolution as in the pressure it exerts on the countryside. The system now in operation favours cereal, to a lesser extent milk production, and, as we have seen, coniferisation in certain areas. Because these are all more profitable than the raising of livestock, farmers – and who can really blame them? – are keen to take advantage of the grants available to convert millions of acres of water meadows, hay meadows, chalk grassland, lowland heath, moorland, and coastal marshes into arable and improved grassland.

What are we losing? Old chalk grassland is characterised by a complicated mixture of plant species that can number as many as 40 per square yard. All these herbs and grasses co-exist because they each exploit the environment in a slightly different way. As well as nurturing many specialised and attractive wild flowers and a wide diversity of birdlife, chalk grassland is notable for butterflies, especially the blues and the skippers. But one application of fertiliser can have a lasting, even permanent effect on plant composition.

Heathland, though generally on poor soil, is particularly important for reptiles and amphibians: all six British reptiles are found in this type of habitat. It is vital for the sand lizard and the smooth snake, and is rich in invertebrates, especially spiders, bees, wasps, and butterflies. About half of Britain's dragonfly species occurs on heathland. It is important, too, for several rare birds such as the red-backed shrike, Dartford warbler, and hobby.

Moorlands and mountains sustain a remarkably rich and varied wildlife and are about the only two types of habitat remaining in Britain where one can find true wilderness. Since 1919 about 2,500,000 acres of moorland have been converted into improved grassland, which is equally destructive of the local flora and fauna.

According to Marion Shoard in *The Theft of the Countryside*, the most damaging change affecting these areas of rough grazing is their conversion to ryegrass monocultures, which is done because 'perennial ryegrass happens to be converted to milk more quickly than any other grass species'. The process involves applying large quantities of lime, fertilisers and pesticides and is especially damaging because it eliminates virtually all plant variety and also the animal life that goes with it. Many species of butterfly, for example, can live on old-style permanent pasture – but not one can live on ryegrass. In the late 1930s, less than two per cent of the permanent grassland was of this type, but by the early 1970s the proportion had jumped to 40 per cent.

Another kind of habitat transformation extremely damaging to wildlife is wetland drainage. Fens, marshes, swamps, bogs, flood-plains, and water meadows are being drained for conversion into yet more farmland. Many of the schemes are carried out by water authorities, mostly supported by funds from the Ministry of Agriculture. The schemes are often expensive: sometimes too expensive. The water authorities are supposed to incorporate in their cost-benefit-analyses some indication of wildlife and landscape values, but they seldom do, because it is very difficult to assign a value to wildlife in the same way as it is to calculate the benefit to farmers.

Along with drainage comes river management, which is also the province of the water authorities. Here the aim is to move water rapidly and efficiently and to prevent flooding. Unfortunately this is of no benefit to wildlife, for such water channels are more like canals than rivers. In *The Common Ground*, Richard Mabey describes the resulting scene:

'Willows and alders are grubbed out to give the excavating machinery room to manoeuvre. Silt dredged from the bottom of the river is dumped on what remains of the bankside vegetation, and the insect life which provides food for fishes and birds has nowhere to breed. The marvellous, complex irregularities that give natural rivers their charm and variety – the meanders and rapids, the pools, eddies, backwaters, shallows, cattle wallows – begin to be levelled out. Otters lose their holts. Kingfishers are unable to find nest sites in the levelled banks. Many water animals begin to decline as their food plants are ripped out and as the water (probably already polluted by sewage) becomes increasingly contaminated by the fertiliser and weedkillers so efficiently drained off the fields. Fish consequently begin to suffer in their turn – but are likely to be declining anyway because the weedy shallows and gravel beds in which they spawn have vanished. Herons, dependent on fish and frogs, have to move away. . . .'

The land-use changes which I have described in this chapter are mainly large-scale ones. But all the time other changes are taking place, which though small in themselves add up to a major loss. Trees and hedges are felled or grubbed out (or sometimes catch fire 'accidentally' during straw-burning). Farm ponds and ditches, so important for amphibians and other smaller forms of life, are filled in because they no longer serve a useful purpose.

The vital wildlife habitat that is disappearing for these various reasons is not necessarily the most remarkable, but is the ordinary habitat of our common species. Furthermore, much of the habitat that still remains is becoming too small and too fragmented to maintain viable populations of certain species, or to act as a reservoir from which other areas can be restocked.

The following summary, prepared by Dr Derek Ratcliffe, Chief Scientist of the Nature Conservancy Council, shows the losses suffered by major habitat types since 1949. For some the scale and rate of loss has been catastrophic.

Lowland herb-rich hay meadows. Probably 95 per cent destroyed, largely by agricultural intensification. Only 3 per cent completely undamaged.

Lowland grassland or sheep walks on chalk and limestone. About 80 per cent destroyed, largely by conversion to arable or improved grassland, with remnants abandoned and suffering deterioration.

Lowland heaths and acidic soils. Probably about 50 to 60 per cent destroyed, largely by conversion to arable or improved grassland, afforestation, or building.

Limestone pavements in Northern England. Probably about 45 per cent damaged or destroyed, largely by removal of weathered surface for sale as rockery stone. Only 3 per cent left completely undamaged.

Ancient lowland woods. Between 30 to 50 per cent destroyed, by conversion to conifer plantations, or by grubbing out to provide more farmland.

Lowland fens, valley and basin mires. Probably about 50 per cent destroyed or significantly damaged by drainage operations, reclamation for agriculture, and chemical enrichment of drainage water.

Lowland raised mires. Probably over 60 per cent destroyed or significantly damaged by afforestation, peat-winning, reclamation for agriculture, or repeated burning.

Upland grasslands, heaths, and mires. Probably about 30 per cent destroyed, mainly by coniferous afforestation, hill land improvement, moor-gripping, and reservoir destruction.

3 Future Options

In the first two chapters we have seen how Britain's countryside, its wildlife and its wild places, have over the centuries been fashioned partly by nature, partly by the hand of man; and how in a matter of decades this natural progression has been irrevocably overturned. The statistics quoted at the end of Chapter 2 indicate the severity of the problem.

Obviously such habitat destruction cannot continue indefinitely at the present rate. The Nature Conservancy Council recently warned that the next decade will be crucial. 'There is increasing public concern about loss of wild animals and plants, and a growing understanding that they depend on suitable habitats for survival. Wildlife is now widely recognised as an integral part of man's whole cultural heritage as well as a vital genetic pool for the future . . .

'There is just about enough habitat left to ensure continuity for Britain's wildlife – if it is conserved. The danger is that, if it is not wholeheartedly protected now, in ten years' time it will be too late.'

The all-important question is – what is being done to tackle the problem?

The Wildlife and Countryside Act provides limited protection for Sites of Special Scientific Interest (SSSIs) of which there are 4,150 (about 900 of them are notable for their geological interest), covering more than 3½ million acres. These SSSIs represent the core of our most valuable habitat. Others are known about but not yet formally designated. Many SSSIs are on National Trust land or form part of other nature reserves and so can be assumed to enjoy favourable protection, regardless of the Act. But for the vast majority the existing safeguards are not very satisfactory.

The principle embodied in the Act is one of voluntary cooperation. If a landowner wishes to carry out changes on an SSSI which may be potentially damaging he is obliged to notify the Nature Conservancy Council. The NCC will then try to reach a 'management agreement' with the landowner, under which he undertakes to manage the site in a non-damaging way. In return, the NCC may well offer him a grant of some kind. If negotiations fail, the only other option open to the NCC is to fall back on its power of compulsory purchase.

It has been estimated that SSSIs are being severely damaged at the rate of five per cent a year, so the question as to how these new arrangements will work in practice is of more than academic interest. At the time of writing (November 1983) the negotiation procedures have not yet been fully tested. Nevertheless, despite repeated assurances from the Government that the necessary funds will be forthcoming, many conservationists fear that the system could prove impossibly expensive to finance.

No one has any idea how much money might be involved, but a clue may be found in rumours that the NCC might have to find £200,000 to prevent a 6,000-acre peat bog in Caithness from being converted to farmland, and £20,000 a year for 65 years to prevent the owner of a Dorset woodland from replacing broadleaved trees with conifers. These sums would represent compensation to the landowners for simply leaving their land as it is.

26

On the positive side, the NCC will at least be forewarned of any damaging changes in land-use which may be planned. Before the passing of the Act, they often had no advance warning and so were unable to influence events.

It might be thought that not all landowners will seek large sums just for doing nothing to their land, but it would be expecting too much of human nature to imagine that they will voluntarily forego money that is there for the asking. It would be rather like telling a gambler which horse was going to win a race and then begging him not to place a bet because it would not be in the interests of the book-maker.

It is often suggested that farmers themselves will want to preserve the quality of their land because they are the natural custodians of the countryside. Regrettably this idealistic view is no longer applicable. The profitability of farming, the advantages of scale, and the huge increase in land values since the war have combined to produce a new kind of farmer. Nowadays farming is more a business than a way of life, and the object of a business is to make money, not to preserve the countryside. Farmland is increasingly being acquired by individuals who have made their money in other spheres, or by large industrial companies, or financial institutions. The same kind of arguments, though different in detail and degree, apply to forestry, which is the other major form of land-use.

In fairness it should be said that not every landowner behaves as if his land were simply a factory whose main function is to produce the maximum profit regardless of other considerations. Many take advantage of the growing network of Farming and Wildlife Advisory Groups which offer advice on how to reconcile the conflicting demands of agriculture and nature conservation. And there are many who are genuinely concerned about the long-term effects of the financial treadmill in which they are trapped.

Earlier in this chapter mention was made of the SSSIs, the sites that are absolutely vital to conservation. However, it would be a bleak prospect if wildlife were to be confined to a network of isolated sanctuaries surrounded by areas which are intensively farmed. If that were to happen the sanctuaries would probably lose their character and would no longer have much meaning. Wildlife should be a natural part of our way of life and not confined in small 'zoos' spread rather thinly across the country.

The big failing of the Wildlife and Countryside Act is that although it protects a range of species from *direct* persecution by man (i.e. killing animals and uprooting plants) it offers little protection against the *indirect* threat of habitat losses, which is of far greater importance to most species. If the top tier of wildlife habitats are only weakly protected, what hope is there for the rest?

Industrialists are beginning to feel that the pattern of Government support is out of balance. They are asking why farmers, who employ a tiny proportion of the working population, are heavily subsidised, while industry, a far bigger employer, is urged to stand on its own feet and be competitive. There are, however, signs that this situation is changing. Late in 1983 the Minister of Agriculture reduced the capital grants available for drainage and some farm buildings, and abolished them altogether for agricultural plant and equipment, hedge removal, and grassland reclamation except in the uplands. (It should be borne in mind that most of the grassland in the lowlands has already been reclaimed.)

One major beneficial change could be made which would not seriously disturb the Wildlife and Countryside Act but which could cost very little. This would be the extension of planning controls to embrace farming and forestry.

When the Town and Country Planning Act was introduced in 1947, it was not thought that these kinds of land-use would be harmful. Indeed, it was felt necessary to protect and encourage them. At that time anxious attention was focussed on such developments as housing, factories, offices, and the proliferation of advertising billboards. In 'Town and Country' planning the word 'Country' is in fact rather misleading, for agricultural landowners may do almost anything they wish without seeking planning consent. Even the construction of farm buildings does not require permission unless they exceed 5,000 square feet in area and 40 feet in height, and are fewer than 100 yards apart or 80 feet from a road.

A change in regulations would ensure that the activities most damaging to wildlife would be subject to public scrutiny and would have to be justified in a way that they are not at present. It would be resented by most farmers and foresters, but there is evidence that a growing minority would accept it, and some would actually welcome its introduction.

There seems to be no very logical reason why most of us in Britain – whether businessmen or private householders – are expected to live within the constraints of planning control, yet one important section of the community has almost complete exemption. Surely in the same way as an old building is listed as being of historic interest and is therefore protected by law, important wildlife areas should be given similar attention. The living countryside is as important a part of our national heritage as are the inanimate reminders of our past. The man who lives in a Tudor manorhouse is very happy to do so and would be most unlikely to want to knock it down and replace it with a modern building: but that is the equivalent of what is happening in the countryside. And when we take into account the fact that much of the destruction is being heavily subsidised with funds supplied by the Ministry of Agriculture and the EEC, we are entitled to question the absurdity of the whole situation. It is as if the Arts Council were to offer grants for the destruction of Constable paintings and their replacement by sculptures made of man-hole covers.

Drainage schemes carried out by water authorities have a particularly damaging effect on wildlife. They are designed to improve agriculture, and they cost the British taxpayer about £150 million a year. The RSPB points out that drainage now threatens to destroy all the remaining flood meadows and grazing marshes in England and Wales, which will be catastrophic for specialised wetland birds such as redshank, snipe, shoveler, yellow wagtail, wigeon, pintail, Bewick's swan, and ruff.

Together with other conservation organisations, the RSPB believes that many of these schemes are a waste of money, regardless of their effect on wildlife. Though the actual benefits of drainage schemes are often over-stated, the public are seldom able to criticise them because both the Ministry of Agriculture and the water authorities claim that the cost-benefit analyses contain confidential information given by the farmers who stand to gain. But should this information really be confidential? Should not the full details be made available to the public who are providing the money?

On rare occasions when the issues are referred to a public enquiry the evidence provided by the authorities is found to be rather suspect. In the celebrated case of Amberley Wildbrooks – a peaceful 1,000-acre haven for wetland wildlife between Pulborough and Arundel which in 1977 the Southern Water Authority wanted to drain – it was found that the figures were distorted and the importance of the area's natural history ignored. The scheme did not go ahead.

In 1983 the Severn-Trent Water Authority put forward a plan to reduce flooding by widening and deepening a 20-mile stretch of the River Soar in Leicestershire.

The scheme was to cost over £6 million and would enable agricultural production to be increased on some 6,700 acres of permanent pasture – buttercup-covered fields separated by hedges and ditches and scattered with numerous small ponds. The Council for the Protection of Rural England and the Leicestershire and Rutland Nature Conservation Trust produced written evidence for a House of Lords select committee which was examining the scheme, pointing out that a severe loss of wildlife habitat was likely to result, as well as a dramatic change in the attractiveness of the landscape. The Water Authority claimed that the scheme would benefit farmers by some £5.8 million, but University of Leeds economist John Bowers (who earlier had exposed serious anomalies in the water authority's case at Amberley Wildbrooks) believed that the figure quoted was greatly over-stated, by as much as £2.5 million.

Water authorities are not always villains. For example, the Anglian Water Authority was persuaded not to lower the water-table in an area of water-filled peat diggings in Suffolk where the rare fen raft spider lives. And there are a number of river management schemes where the authorities work with conservation organisations to achieve the minimum disturbance to wildlife. But on the whole their commitment to conservation seems small.

One reason may lie in the way in which water authority board membership is constituted. In 1981 the Department of the Environment announced that the government would try to appoint men and women with conservation experience – but a couple of years later the Department admitted that this was no longer the government's intention.

Even if it proves possible to achieve a significant slowing down of the rate at which marginal land is converted to intensive agriculture, we are left with the problem of how to maintain its character as a haunt for wildlife. As we have seen, much of this land was fashioned by traditional farming methods. It would be unreasonable to expect farmers to pay for the maintenance of hedgerows which they don't need or to clear scrub from downs that are no longer grazed.

A vast reservoir of enthusiasm exists in the voluntary movement for carrying out tasks such as hedging and ditching, the construction and maintenance of dry stone walls, and pond and scrub clearance. Given a modest amount of public money, especially to pay for tools, transport, and other out-of-pocket expenses, this effort could be greatly expanded. The major organisation in the field is the British Trust for Conservation Volunteers, but many others, including the county conservation trusts, also carry out work of this kind. Such co-operation for mutual benefit would do much to reconcile farmers and conservationists, who are at present increasingly separated by a barrier of antagonism.

Some comparatively minor adjustments could be made – either by amending the Wildlife and Countryside Act or by other means – which would be of important benefit to certain species.

Amphibians and reptiles receive very summary treatment in the Act compared with birds. Of the twelve species listed, eight are protected 'in respect of trade only'. But it appears that licences are being freely issued to dealers wishing to collect and sell these species, without enquiry as to the numbers involved or where they will be caught. The statistics will be reviewed after a few years – but they will cover only the number actually sold, and many of the creatures will probably die before they are sold. Some if not all of these species could be given full protection without great inconvenience to anyone. How many people, after all, really want to or need to keep snakes, toads, or lizards as pets? Full protection would help the smooth snake because at present people can kill it and claim that they thought it was an adder or a grass snake.

Every spring between the hours of 7 and 10pm there are many casualties among toads crossing roads to reach their breeding ponds. In Europe there is extensive publicity in certain places, including road signs, warning motorists to be on the alert for toad traffic. Tunnels have even been built under German autobahns to help the toads to get across safely. In Britain there are some springtime 'toad patrols' which try to help the animals, but it is important that they should know exactly what they are doing. In some cases well-meaning people have picked up toads and carried them back to the side of the road from whence they came, instead of to where they were going. It might be worth paying attention to the more advanced techniques in use in Europe.

Certain birds are subject to unintentional disturbance by picnickers, bird-watchers, and other visitors. Species affected include the black-throated diver, the Slavonian grebe, and the dotterel. This problem could be solved by judicious zoning of popular tourist areas to cordon off the vulnerable birds. It might only be necessary at certain times of the year.

Apart from the bats, mammals do not feature much in the schedules of the Act. Some, it is true, receive a degree of protection by the prohibition of most methods of killing except shooting. But how many people are really likely to shoot dormice or shrews? Why not give them and animals such as the pine marten, polecat, wild cat and hedgehog a full listing? Unfortunately quite a lot of people still think of mammals as pests, which may be why they are only given reluctant protection compared with birds and plants.

For years conservation bodies have been lobbying governments to establish some publicly funded system to enforce wildlife legislation, but even now that the Wildlife and Countryside Act extends statutory protection to a much wider range of animals and plants than ever before, enforcement remains a rather hit and miss affair. The RSPB and RSPCA do splendid work in bringing offenders to court, especially in connection with wild birds, but there is little official activity.

As the police have so many other problems to contend with it is not surprising that they do not go out of their way to track down miscreants who raid birds' nests or who pick wild flowers unlawfully. Yet it does not seem fair that the onus should rest almost entirely on charitable organisations. In the USA the Fish and Wildlife Service employs a staff of enforcement officers who investigate the worst offences. We in Britain should find the money to do the same.

In the past, bodies such as the RSPB felt justifiably frustrated when their efforts to bring offenders to court were thwarted by magistrates imposing only paltry fines. The position is now different, and heavy fines, often near the maximum allowable, are handed out to egg-thieves and those who take young birds of prey. In late 1983, for instance, Lerwick Sheriff's Court fined two men £1,300 and £1,000 respectively for taking eggs. They were caught as they were about to leave Shetland with 80 eggs, including those of the red-throated diver and the whimbrel. Other recent sentences include a £900 fine for taking a peregrine falcon and eggs, and £795 for illegal trapping of finches. Also, a Belgian who tried to smuggle four goshawks through Felixstowe Docks was fined £300.

There are a number of other indications that there may still be hope for our wild-life. According to a recent MORI opinion poll commissioned by a conservation consortium 'to find out about British attitudes to resource use and the environment', 53% of those questioned believe that attractive countryside makes a valuable contribution to the quality of life. Wildlife in the countryside, and gardens, were considered important by 37%.

There has certainly been a notable improvement in dealing with pollution, of which the purifying of the Thames is an outstanding example: over 100 species of fish have now been recorded along its reaches. Recently a six-pound-two-ounce salmon was caught with a rod and line near Chertsey – the first time this has happened since 1833.

During the 1950s and 1960s pesticide pollution was a major threat to many species, especially those at the ends of food chains such as the birds of prey. But since those days enormous improvements have been made by pesticide manufacturers, which have resulted in either the phasing out of many of the most toxic or long-lasting compounds, or in severe restriction on their use. Since dieldrin was withdrawn from use in sheep-dips in 1966 there has been a marked improvement in the breeding success of the golden eagle. Also, DDT has been withdrawn from many major uses in both agriculture and horticulture.

Insecticides and herbicides can still kill – that is what they are designed to do (and of course, modern farming requires their use to achieve maximum efficiency). But they are far less of a problem than they used to be. As well as improved chemicals, economics, too, are having an effect, with cash shortages causing many councils to reduce or discontinue their expenditure on chemical sprays. As a result, roadside verges are coming back into bloom in a spectacular way.

Some of the plants that benefit may be species that come into the category of 'weeds' (one definition of a weed is a wild flower that occurs where it is not wanted). It is encouraging to find the gardening correspondent of *The Times* urging his readers to accommodate wild flowers in their gardens: 'I would like to suggest that whenever possible areas which can be left to grow quite naturally should be allowed to do so.' He says that some wild flowers are very beautiful, but slightly detracts from the point by adding that they 'would almost compete with some of the hybrids raised for the bedding schemes in parks'. Many botanists would put it the other way round.

Although it is not yet possible to re-create ancient meadows and grasslands over a reasonable time-scale, promising research by NCC scientists shows that carefully selected seed mixtures can nevertheless produce artificial habitats that are remarkably rich in wild flowers. At this stage of research there are, of course, problems, notably the fact that most commercial seedsmen concentrate on species in demand for agriculture and horticulture, and many of their mixtures may contain seeds of foreign origin. Care must be taken to plant the right mixtures in the right area; random planting is seldom satisfactory.

But local authorities are already showing great interest in using the seed mixtures in places such as wasteland, the ground around factories, roadside verges, and parks. A few specialist seedsmen have even started selling 'conservation mixtures' of native British grasses and wild flowers.

Re-establishing orchids in the wild is even more complicated; it is notoriously difficult to grow them from seed, and even transplants rarely survive. Recently, however, there has been a revival of hope for Britain's wild orchids, many of which are severely reduced. The breakthrough has come through the work of Dr Mark Clements, an Australian botanist working at Kew Gardens. His research reveals that as orchids grow in close association with particular species of fungus their seeds will not germinate unless infected by the correct fungus, which supplies essential nutrients.

Having first identified the correct fungus species, Dr Clements then places it, with the orchid seed, in a growing medium of oats, water, and agar. In about nine months the orchid seedlings are ready to transplant in the wild, together with their fungus, which is by now integrated in the plant. One possible benefit of the technique is that it will enable commercial growers to make available a variety of orchid species, thus removing the desire of collectors to seek them in the wild.

As well as the rehabilitation of plants, animals can also be reintroduced to areas where they have become extinct. As mentioned elsewhere in this book, the white-tailed eagle has already been brought back to Scotland, and there are plans to reintroduce the large blue butterfly. The Otter Trust has released three captive-bred otters in Suffolk and hopes to release more if the project is successful. A long-running scheme to reintroduce the great bustard in southern England has so far proved unsuccessful, but hope has not been abandoned. Another group plans to release beavers, if an area of suitable habitat can be found. (Under the Act, a licence is now necessary to reintroduce species which are extinct in Britain.)

There is much that individuals can do to help wildlife. Landowners who enjoy shooting pheasants maintain thousands of acres in a natural state to provide cover for the birds, and in doing so provide habitat for many other animals and plants. This is very often land that it would otherwise be more profitable to farm or replant with conifers.

The heath fritillary is an interesting example of a woodland creature threatened by seemingly inexorable habitat destruction. It flourishes in coppice, but in Kent most of this has been turned into commercial forest. Suitable sites are increasingly isolated, and the butterfly is less able to find coppice in the right condition. In fact, if the pulp mill at Sittingbourne were to close down, the coppice market in the area would collapse entirely, probably bringing about the demise of the heath fritillary in that part of England.

Its future may be more hopeful in Cornwall, thanks to HRH The Prince of Wales. In consultation with the NCC and the Cornwall Trust for Nature Conservation, he arranged for 20 acres of newly planted conifers in the Tamar Valley to be uprooted in order to manage the area for the heath fritillary – which already since then appears to be on the increase.

The Prince has recently set aside a small area to protect the butterfly orchid, reinstating dry-stone walls, and planting trees and hedgerows. He also hopes to see established in the Scillies a new National Nature Reserve, covering all the uncultivated land and all the uninhabited islands, as well as one of the first Marine Nature Reserves. He encourages enlightened systems of land management throughout the Duchy of Cornwall, seeing this as an opportunity to prove that profitable farming can be compatible with conservation.

While landowners and farmers have a large-scale influence – either good or bad – in conserving our wildlife, on a smaller scale it is a matter which affects millions of us. Conservation cannot be successful without widespread public support. The more people who participate in it, at whatever level, the better chance we have of saving our wildlife, and there are a variety of possibilities open to anyone interested. On pages 198 to 203 of this book we provide a list of many of the organisations which exist to study, protect, and conserve our natural heritage.

Flora

Small alison   *Alyssum alyssoides*

The small alison is a low-growing annual herb of the cabbage family. It is generally found in grassy fields and arable land, especially where the turf is short and open. Its tiny flowers, which appear from April to June, contain very little nectar and are seldom visited by insects.

It was introduced to this country from Europe, and though it grows well across a wide area around the Mediterranean, in Britain it is confined largely to the Brecklands and the Sandlings in Suffolk. It has been seen in other locations as far afield as Scotland, but these are now thought to have been rare occurrences.

Like many flowers of the English countryside, the small alison was badly affected by the advent of herbicide spraying, particularly during the 1970s, when drifting chemicals destroyed many plants. It is not protected by any specific conservation measures and is classified as endangered.

Bedstraw broomrape *Orobanche caryophyllacea*

Broomrapes are a family of parasites. They attach themselves at the seedling stage to the young roots of other plants, which they penetrate in order to receive their food. They have no leaves and no green pigment, only a thick, fleshy, flowering stem.

The bedstraw broomrape is so named because its host plant is the hedge bedstraw. It was first discovered growing on the chalky soil of the North Downs by G. E. Smith at the end of the eighteenth century. According to Smith the flowers 'when newly expanded, distil a fragrant scent of cloves', hence its other name of 'clove-scented broomrape'. The flowers appear in June and July and are particularly attractive to bees.

It is fairly common in Europe but in this country it is definitely known to grow only near the coast in south-east Kent. (There is a possibility that it once grew in Argyll but this is unconfirmed.) Although the Kent population of the bedstraw broomrape is not large, it has a degree of protection since it occurs in two areas that are designated Sites of Special Scientific Interest (SSSI). It is nevertheless classified as endangered.

Oxtongue broomrape   *Orobanche loricata*

Broomrapes can differ in appearance depending on their host plant. This makes them difficult to recognise individually, and the easiest way is to identify the plant on which they are growing. The oxtongue broomrape grows on the roots of hawksbeards and oxtongues, particularly the hawkweed oxtongue.

Unlike the common broomrape, it has very hairy stamens. It is abundant only in one location in Kent, but has also been found growing at a site in Somerset. Earlier records suggest that it was once more widely distributed in the Home Counties, and as far afield as Brecon, Worcestershire and Guernsey, but the accuracy of some of these identifications is doubtful. It also occurs in Europe.

Since all broomrapes depend for survival on the chance of their seeds falling by a host plant, the numbers can fluctuate greatly. It is probably for this reason, and because of over-zealous collecting, that they are so scarce. The oxtongue broomrape is protected in one SSSI and is classified as endangered.

Thistle broomrape   *Orobanche reticulata*

A nineteenth-century botanist claimed that any of the broomrapes could be made to grow in the garden, on gorse or broom. Sadly this seems unlikely in view of the preference of most British broomrapes for very specific host plants, such as various thistles of the genera *Cirsium* and *Carduus*.

Though the thistle broomrape grows only on magnesian limestone, it was at one time quite common. Now it is restricted to four localities in Yorkshire. In one of these areas alone, just before the Second World War, 400 spikes were recorded; by the late 1960s there were fewer than 10. It is also rare in the other three locations.

It grows to a height of between 12 and 20 inches, and the flowers, which have no scent, appear during July. It is endangered by threats from ploughing, chemical spraying, dumping and gravel working, and is further threatened by the Weeds Act of 1959. One of its host plants, the creeping thistle, is a notifiable weed under this Act, and farmers are obliged to destroy it on their land. This inevitably kills any of the parasitic broomrapes that may be living on the thistle.

The species is protected in one Nature Reserve.

Wood calamint   *Calamintha sylvatica*

The wood calamint is a perennial of the thyme family, with mint-scented leaves (which are larger than those of the common calamint), and flowers that are borne from July to September. It is native to the Isle of Wight and its site there on a chalky bank is the only known location in Britain. It is not certain why it has become so scarce, but a Nature Reserve has been established for its protection. It is now listed as vulnerable in this country, though, as is often the case, it is still quite widely distributed throughout Europe.

It used to be said that if you put calamint leaves on meat that had gone slightly off, they would remove 'all unpleasant odours and flavour'. Perhaps this gave rise to the custom of serving mint sauce with lamb. The calamints were also once thought to contain an antidote to snake bites.

Alpine catchfly   *Lychnis alpina*

The alpine catchfly is a short, tufted perennial and a member of the pink family. Its dense clusters of deep pink flowers appear in June and July and are particularly attractive to butterflies. This is a sub-Arctic and alpine species that is found on bare mountains in Europe, Asia and North America. It tends to grow only in soils which have a high content of heavy metals such as copper, zinc and nickel.

It was at one time to be found in Westmorland but it has since disappeared from there. The two remaining sites are both in Cumberland, where the small population is confined to two remote gullies in the Lake District; and in Angus, where it is more numerous but nevertheless still in decline. Both populations have suffered from excessive collecting.

As it occurs in one Nature Reserve its status is listed as vulnerable rather than endangered.

Rock cinquefoil *Potentilla rupestris*

This member of the rose family was first recorded in 1688. Its common name comes from the French 'cinque feuilles', five leaves, because its flower is made up of five petals. It is a perennial, growing to a height of between six and twelve inches, and blooms in May and June. Though found throughout Europe and North America, in Britain it is confined to four locations in Mid-Wales and Northern Scotland. It favours basic rocks such as limestone.

Having been so heavily collected from one of the locations in Wales it was thought to have become extinct, until a few plants were found on the same site thirty-five years ago. Elsewhere in Wales it is under constant threat from quarry excavations and blasting.

In the far north of Scotland there is one large colony scattered thickly over an isolated cliff; it is to be hoped that the site is sufficiently remote to deter collectors.

The species is protected in one SSSI and is listed as vulnerable.

Triangular club-rush   *Scirpus triquetrus*

This stout perennial rush is found along the muddy banks of tidal rivers. It grows to a height of three to four feet, and its name is derived from its sharply triangular stem and club-like inflorescence (the part of the plant that consists of flower-bearing stalks). It now occurs only in the estuary of the River Tamar between Devon and Cornwall. Several small populations are known, though the species is not protected in Nature Reserves.

It was once found in several places in the Home Counties, especially along the Thames and its tributaries, but has disappeared, apparently as a result of the building of embankments. But it is still thriving in Ireland, where it is common along a stretch of the River Shannon. It is also widespread elsewhere, occurring in Europe, Asia, Africa, and North America.

Another British club-rush, the round-headed, is also a rare species. It occurs on damp, sandy flats by the sea in Devon (where there is a large and well-protected population) and in Somerset (where the population is very small). Both club-rushes belong to the same genus as the true bulrush.

Wild cotoneaster *Cotoneaster integerrimus*

The wild cotoneaster is a deciduous shrub of the rose family growing on limestone rocks, mainly in upland regions. In exposed areas its knotted, sparsely-leaved stems hardly rise above the ground and it rarely exceeds three feet, but when sheltered from the wind it may reach five feet. Its pinkish flowers appear from April to June and are followed in the autumn by bright red berries, as in this photograph.

It is one of Britain's rarest plants and is found only at one hill site in Caernarvonshire. This scattered colony was once relatively numerous, but by 1900 had become virtually extinct. Now just four plants are known to exist. It also grows in Europe, from Scandinavia to Spain, and eastwards to Iran, but is scarce everywhere.

Several related cotoneaster species have been introduced to Britain from India and China and though they are commonly found in gardens, some of them have established themselves in the wild.

The present perilous status of the wild cotoneaster in Britain results from a combination of browsing by goats and sheep, and by over-collecting. The four surviving plants occur in an SSSI, and the species is classified as endangered.

Note As we go to press we learn that a local conservation programme has resulted in a substantial increase in the number of plants.

Field cow-wheat *Melampyrum arvense*

Once fairly common in Southern and Eastern England, the field cow-wheat is now restricted to about six locations in the Isle of Wight, Essex and Bedfordshire. It is an annual weed and because its favoured habitat is cornfields on chalky soil it has become endangered almost entirely as a result of modern agricultural methods: a combination of stubble-burning, the use of herbicides, the destruction of hedges, and the filling in of ditches.

The flowers, unlike those of the common cow-wheat (which are yellow), are dark pink with a touch of yellow. They appear between June and September.

The generic name, *Melampyrum*, comes from two Greek words meaning 'black' and 'wheat', and indeed the seeds look like blackish wheat grains. Bread made from flour containing field cow-wheat seeds tastes rather bitter. In the Isle of Wight the plant was once so abundant that it contaminated all the wheat and made the bread unmarketable. Because of this it became known locally as 'Poverty Weed'.

As no special conservation measures have been taken, the field cow-wheat is now seriously endangered.

Jersey cudweed   *Gnaphalium luteoalbum*

The Jersey cudweed is a short to medium annual herb of the daisy family that grows in sand dunes, sandy fields, and waste places. Its stem and short flower-bearing branches – which bloom from July to September – are covered with white, woolly hairs. It is native to both Jersey and Guernsey, where it still occurs, and to Norfolk, where it was not seen for a decade and was thought to have become extinct, until a large population was discovered in 1978. Plants have also been recorded occasionally in other parts of Southern and Eastern England, but they may have been introduced rather than indigenous, as they never seemed to establish themselves for more than a year or two in these locations.

Its decline is thought to be due to changing agricultural practices, especially the introduction of herbicides. However, it is found in many other temperate parts of the world, in particular those areas where there is little or no herbicide spraying.

The cudweeds derive their name not from the cud that cows chew, but from the word 'cut'. In the past the soft hairs from the stems of cudweed were used as a bandage-lining to prevent chafing.

The population of Jersey cudweeds is declining and vulnerable.

Diapensia   *Diapensia lapponica*

This attractive evergreen flowering shrub was recorded for the first time in Britain in July 1951; whether it had been present for long before, or was indeed a newcomer, is a matter for conjecture. The first person to see it was an amateur ornithologist who was exploring a barren mountain-top in Inverness-shire that had been of no interest to botanists. The diapensia is still known to exist only in this one site, where it grows at a height of approximately 2,600 feet, in an area no larger than an acre or two. It is widespread in Arctic regions of Europe and North America.

Its pretty, pale yellow flowers, which appear in May, grow from rosettes that are densely packed into 'cushions' sometimes several feet across. The centre of the cushion is inclined to die out and is replaced by young cushions that in time spread over surrounding areas of barren ground. Marjorie Blamey reports that the famous Scottish naturalist Seton Gordon once found a thermometer near a diapensia and feared it indicated that some collector wanted to find out the most suitable conditions for growing this rare species. It certainly is collected to some extent, in spite of its inaccessibility.

Field eryngo *Eryngium campestre*

This prickly perennial herb of the carrot family grows in dry grassy places on limestone and chalk, usually near the coast. Its yellowy-white, thistle-like flowers appear in July and August.

It was once widespread in Southern England from Cornwall to Suffolk, but is now restricted to Devon, Hampshire, Kent and Guernsey, and has been successfully reintroduced to Wiltshire.

The probable reason for its sharp decline in this century is that the fields where it grew have been ploughed up. Of the existing locations, two in Devon are said to contain large and increasing populations and to be well protected. It also occurs in drier areas of Europe, in North Africa, and in parts of Asia.

The name eryngo comes from the Greek word meaning to belch, and herbalists recommended both the field eryngo and its close relative, the sea holly, for relieving indigestion. Its roots were considered to have many other remarkable properties and were prescribed for a range of conditions. The sixteenth-century herbalist John Gerard recommended it for 'people that are consumed and withered with age and who want natural moisture'. A later practitioner, Nicholas Culpepper, claimed that the root was good for the liver and spleen, for jaundice, dropsy, pain in the loins, wind and colic and an assortment of urinary malfunctions.

Dickie's bladder fern   *Cystopteris dickieana*

This slender, vividly green fern with its almost transparent fronds was once found in several isolated sea-caves on the coast of North-East Scotland, where it was discovered by a Dr Dickie in 1846. It has now disappeared from two of its known locations in Perthshire, but a substantial number are still to be found in a cave in Kincardineshire. Environmental changes inside this cave seem to cause a natural fluctuation in the number of plants, which like deep shade.

Though some fern species are much prized by collectors, there is no particular evidence that Dickie's bladder fern has been subject to depredation. Its remaining location lies within an SSSI.

The species is closely related to the brittle bladder fern, from which it can be distinguished only by examination of its spores. There is therefore a possibility that after further research Dickie's bladder fern might be found to have a wider distribution. A fern with identical physical appearance has, for example, been collected in Cornwall. Elsewhere the species is found in Arctic regions of Europe and Asia.

Killarney fern *Trichomanes speciosum*

As its name suggests, this fern was, and is, more abundant in South-West Ireland than in Britain. However, it does occur in a few places in South-West and North-West England, Wales, and Scotland. It grows among rocks in well-shaded and very humid places, and is in bloom from July to September.

The botanist Anne Pratt saw the fern in Ireland in the nineteenth century, and noted the 'rich verdant drapery formed by its masses on the wet rock'. She said that 'the guide at Turk Rock near Killarney has sold so many that it is almost exterminated in that spot'. Initially it was difficult to grow in cul-tivation, but eventually a Mr N. B. Ward was successful and proudly showed the result to Baron Fischer, the Emperor of Russia's botanical superintendent. The Baron is reported to have taken off his hat, bowed deeply to the fern, and said: 'You have been my master all the days of my life.'

In Britain the number of sites is unknown, but most populations have been seriously reduced by the depredations of collectors. In Ireland, it is now, for the same reason, confined to inaccessible places. It is also found in Europe.

Brown galingale   *Cyperus fuscus*

This rather small and inconspicuous annual sedge grows in damp places, especially bare ground left by the drying up of ponds and ditches. Once found in various parts of Southern England, it is now in serious decline and is restricted to Somerset, Hampshire, and Middlesex. Only one of the three remaining populations is of any size and even this tends to fluctuate from year to year. The decline of the species is due to the elimination of its rather specialised habitat, probably through drainage and change of land-use.

Its name may come from an Arabic word, in turn derived from a Chinese word meaning mild ginger. It was applied to the galingales because of their rather bitter-tasting roots, which are succulent and aromatic and are considered by herbalists to have many useful properties, among them the relief of giddiness. A related species produces underground tubers that in Europe are called 'tiger nuts' and are used in the making of iced drinks. Sedges such as the galingale tend to dominate boggy places but arouse little interest among botanists because their flowers are mostly small and wind-pollinated.

Alpine gentian *Gentiana nivalis*

The alpine gentian is an upright, slender annual that grows on rock ledges between 2,400 and 3,400 feet above sea-level. It is one of the rarest mountain plants in Britain, found only at eight sites in Perthshire and Angus, on the southern edge of the Scottish Highlands.

It is variable in height: some plants standing only an inch or two, while in sheltered spots others may reach six inches. The flowers, which appear in July and August, are about half the size of the spring gentian, though they are of the same brilliant blue. The number of flowers on each plant can be as many as twenty, and in common with other members of the gentian family they open only in bright sunshine.

Not many British mountain plants are annuals, which have to germinate, produce flowers, then seed all in one season. If the summer growing season is short and the weather conditions are adverse, germination is severely restricted. The alpine gentian population therefore fluctuates quite considerably from year to year. Furthermore, in spite of its habitat some sites are accessible to collectors, who are to a large degree responsible for the decline in numbers.

The species also occurs in Europe and North America.

Spring gentian *Gentiana verna*

The spring gentian (so called because it flowers from April to June) is a perennial growing on limestone in sandy, grassy and rather damp areas. A true alpine plant of great beauty, it is found at heights between 1,200 and 2,500 feet in the Pennine Hills, where Yorkshire, Durham, Westmorland and Cumberland meet.

It still seems to be fairly prolific, though in a comparatively small area. More than fifty locations are known and about forty of the populations are in a National Nature Reserve. However, in some places it is declining and undoubtedly suffers heavily from large-scale collecting. The culprits are mostly selfish gardeners who cannot be bothered to visit an alpine nursery. As Marjorie Blamey has said, 'With a little care and patience any gardener can grow these flowers and collect his own seed to ensure a succession of plants.'

The spring gentian also grows in Western Ireland, though at lower altitudes, from sea-level up to 1,000 feet. It is abundant in the high pastures of Europe and Asia.

Water germander   *Teucrium scordium*

The water germander is a perennial herb which grows along the banks of rivers and ditches on calcareous soils and on dune slacks. It varies in height from between three to twelve inches. Its leaves are softly hairy, their texture seeming to vary according to the location; the uninitiated might mistake them for nettles. The pale purple flowers appear from July onwards.

The species was once quite widely distributed over an area stretching down from Yorkshire to Southern England and the Channel Islands. Nowadays it appears to be confined to three locations in Devon and Cambridgeshire; it was reintroduced to one of them after being extinct for several years. Another possible location is in Lincolnshire, though no evidence has been recorded there recently. Its decline in England is almost entirely due to drainage and land reclamation.

It was once considered to have medicinal qualities and was used as a cure for various infectious diseases. Like the wood germander and the wood sage, its leaves smell like garlic.

It is fairly abundant in Western Ireland, especially along the banks of the River Shannon.

Wild gladiolus *Gladiolus illyricus*

The wild gladiolus is a perennial of the iris family, and grows among bracken and gorse on bushy heathlands.

It is now found only in Hampshire, although in the past it also grew on the Isle of Wight (from where it vanished in 1897), and was recorded as an introduction in Devon and the Channel Islands. It is of Mediterranean origin and is still found in Europe, especially in the south. One or two similar species of gladiolus from Europe have been grown in gardens in Britain and have subsequently seeded themselves and reverted to their wild state. They include the field gladiolus (*Gladiolus segetum*) and eastern gladiolus (*Gladiolus byzantium*).

Growing to about a foot in height, it is more delicate in shape and texture, as well as being smaller, than the familiar garden variety. Unfortunately its beauty seems to prove irresistible to picnickers, especially when it grows in the vicinity of car parks.

According to Perring and Farrell about forty populations of the wild gladiolus are known, though some of these may have been planted. It is encouraging to note that a recent field study has revealed a wider distribution than was previously estimated.

Sickle-leaved hare's-ear   *Bupleurum falcatum*

This perennial was first discovered in 1831 in Essex, scattered over a broad area between Ongar and Chelmsford. It is a member of the carrot family and grows to a height of between one and three feet. The flowers are a deep yellow and appear from July to September. It tends to grow on waste land and in grassy places, especially banks under hedges.

It is possible that this plant was introduced to Britain from abroad, and it still flourishes in Europe, Asia and Japan.

Thirty years ago it was restricted to one short stretch of damp verge and ditch-bank, but in 1962 the site was destroyed by hedgerow clearance and ditch-cleaning. It was therefore considered extinct, until 1979, when a single plant was found at the same site. According to Perring and Farrell, seed from this plant was taken to a nature reserve of the Essex Naturalists' Trust, and from it a population has been successfully established. It can hardly be regarded as secure, however, and remains one of the most endangered of Britain's wild plants.

Small hare's-ear   *Bupleurum baldense*

The small hare's-ear is a low-growing annual that seldom reaches even as much as four inches in height – its tiny yellow flowers measuring barely a tenth of an inch across. It favours limestone, growing on dry banks, rocky slopes, chalk cliffs and grey dunes near the sea. It is inconspicuous and therefore difficult to find, except, perhaps, after a wet spring, when it may be two or three times larger than it is during a dry season.

Never very widespread on the mainland, it is now confined to two locations, one in Devon and the other in Sussex. It has also been recorded as a casual in Surrey, Leicestershire and Yorkshire. It occurs in all the main Channel Islands except Sark, and is found in Southern Europe as far east as Italy.

A third species of hare's-ear, the thorow-wax (*B. rotundifolium*), has almost certainly become extinct in recent times. It grew in cornfields, mainly on chalk, and declined rapidly in the 1920s after the introduction of cleaner seed corn.

Blue heath *Phyllodoce caerulea*

This low-growing, bushy, evergreen undershrub is found on rocky moorlands in Scotland at a height of around 2,400 feet. It is difficult to understand quite how it came to be called 'blue' (the Latin name translated means 'sky blue'). Various authors describe the colour of its flowers as 'pink', 'purple', and in one case 'purplish-pink tinged with blue'. It is sometimes more appropriately referred to as the 'mountain heath' and has also been called the Scottish menziesia.

The blue heath does not always flower during its short summer season and it does not consistently produce seed, but maintains itself mainly by putting out runners. This ensures some protection from collectors, as does the fact that its leaves resemble those of crowberry, another heath-like evergreen undershrub. Unfortunately it is occasionally trampled on by hill walkers ignorant of its rarity.

The species is known from two very small colonies in Inverness-shire and four sites in Perthshire. On one Perthshire site, where it was first recorded, it has been subjected to raids by botanists and gardeners for over 150 years.

Red helleborine   *Cephalanthera rubra*

This perennial orchid is found only in beechwoods on limestone soils. It grows to a height of two feet. The flowers appear from May to early August and do not open very wide, though more fully than those of closely-related species. As they need sunlight but are generally confined to shaded places in dense woodland, only a small proportion of the plants produce blooms. However, by spreading underground they can propagate new colonies.

In Britain the species is now found only in the Chiltern Hills in Buckinghamshire and the Cotswold Hills in Gloucestershire. In the past it was recorded in several other southern English counties, but was probably never very abundant. It is also found in Central and Southern Europe and in North Africa, sometimes in large colonies.

When it is not in flower its green leaves are deceptively similar to those of the more common large white helleborine; it takes an expert to distinguish one from the other. It has long been prized by flower hunters, attracted by its rarity and pretty blooms. It is an endangered species, but occurs in two reserves, one of them a National Nature Reserve.

Perennial knawel *Scleranthus perennis*

The perennial knawel is a low-growing herb of the pink family that closely resembles its relative, the annual knawel, though it is usually more robust. Its flowers, which have no petals, are small but more conspicuous than those of the annual species.

This plant generally grows on rather bare ground, dry sandy heaths, and abandoned arable fields. It is also found in Southern Scandinavia, Central and Southern Europe, and Western Asia.

In Britain there are two sub-species. *S.p. perennis* is found in only one isolated and rocky locality in Radnorshire. Its numbers fluctuate considerably, and in some years it is reduced to just one plant. *S.p. prostratus* is an endemic sub-species that grows on sandy heaths in the Brecklands of Suffolk, where there are four colonies. In the past it also occurred in Norfolk.

The Radnor sub-species is constantly threatened by collectors and holiday visitors, the East Anglian sub-species by agricultural and housing development. The Radnor knawel occurs within a National Nature Reserve.

Some of the Breckland plants are protected in an SSSI and are of particular importance, as they are found only in Britain.

Sea knotgrass *Polygonum maritimum*

Sea knotgrass is a perennial member of the dock family and is found on sand and fine shingle at, and just above, the spring tide high-water level. Its flowers appear in August and September.

It is now known at two locations in Cornwall, and at Herm in the Channel Islands, where it has become sparse. It was formerly recorded in the Isles of Scilly, Devon, Somerset and Hampshire; also in Glamorganshire, where it had been introduced.

Outside Britain it has recently been discovered in Ireland, and it is also found in South-Western Europe and the Mediterranean.

There is no particular reason for the sea knotgrass's rarity, although its distribution pattern suggests that it is on the edge of its range in this country. Fluctuations in distribution are characteristic of strand-line species, and it is possible that the population may increase again. It does not occur in any nature reserve.

Sea lavender *Limonium paradoxum* and *Limonium recurvum*

These members of the sea lavender family (which also includes thrift) are short, hairless perennials. Apart from the colour of the flowers, they have no connection with true lavender, and are in fact scentless. They are allied to rock sea lavender, *L. binervosum*, which, according to the nineteenth-century botanist G. E. Smith, 'appears under as great a variety of names as a Spanish grandee'.

L. paradoxum and *L. recurvum* are characterised by having flowers on all but the lowest branches, and bloom from July to September. They occur on maritime rocks and cliffs.

Over a hundred plants of *L. paradoxum* have been counted in its one remaining site in Pembrokeshire. It can also be found in East Donegal. *L. recurvum* now only grows in a single location in Dorset. Although this is a healthy population, it is under pressure from a nearby camping ground.

These are the only two members of the sea lavender family to be listed in the Wildlife and Countryside Act, though a third, *L. transwallianum*, is almost as rare, being confined to two locations in Pembrokeshire.

Limonium recurvum

Round-headed leek *Allium sphaerocephalon*

The round-headed leek is a bulbous perennial standing as high as two feet six inches. It is closely related to garlic, onion, chive and ramsons, and has a similar smell; in fact an old name for this species was 'small round-headed garlic'.

It is found in grassy places among limestone rocks and on sand dunes. Its flowers, which grow in globular heads, appear from June to August.

In Britain it occurs within a National Nature Reserve on limestone cliffs on the Gloucestershire side of the Avon Gorge, where it was first discovered in 1847. There are two separate colonies. One of them is small, consisting of some ten plants, but is reasonably secure. The other is large, but unfortunately is in an area accessible to collectors; it has also been damaged by schoolchildren from Bristol as they clamber over the rocks.

There is a small population of round-headed leeks on the Channel Island of Jersey. It is just managing to survive, though as it is near the sea, it too is under pressure from visitors.

The species is also found in much of Europe and Central Russia.

Least lettuce   *Lactuca saligna*

The least lettuce is an annual, some-times biennial, herb of the daisy family. Its slender wavy stem may be from one to three feet tall. It usually grows near the sea in bare grassy places, in salt-marshes, on shingle and on sea walls. The flowers appear in July and August. The plant bears no resemblance to the garden lettuce; its scientific name *lactuca* means 'containing milk'.

The species was once quite wide-spread, mainly in South-East England. There are records from Sussex, Kent, Essex, Middlesex, Suffolk, Norfolk, Cambridgeshire and Huntingdonshire. It disappeared from Middlesex in about 1800, and gradually declined elsewhere until by the 1960s it occurred in only nine places, in Sussex, Kent and Essex. However at one Essex location in 1978 nearly 7,000 plants were counted. The reasons for its overall decline in Eng-land are not clear, but are probably due to the alteration or destruction of its habitat, such as the improvement of sea defences. It is protected in one locally-administered nature reserve, and is classified as endangered.

Abroad, it is found from Northern Europe to the Mediterranean.

Wild lettuce was credited with a wide and contradictory range of powers. As late as the last century it was believed that if it was eaten during the day it would calm the mind and allay nervous irritability. If eaten in the evening it would help combat insomnia (one of its old names was 'sleepwort').

Snowdon lily *Lloydia serotina*

The Snowdon lily is a perennial member of the lily family which grows in grassy places among rocks. It is a small plant, about six inches tall, with a slender stem. In common with many of its relatives, it has a bulb to help it survive the winter. Most such plants grow in warm regions, especially in Southern Europe, but this particular species is unusual in that it thrives at around 1,500 to 2,500 feet. Its single, crocus-like flowers appear in May.

It is widespread in the mountains of Europe, Asia and North America, but in Britain it is found only on basic rock ledges in the mountains of Snowdonia in North Wales; there were once twelve sites, but these have now dwindled to five. Though usually a solitary plant, it sometimes occurs in groups of up to a hundred.

Its initial decline was brought about by collectors, but a more recent threat has been the popularity of Snowdonia among climbers and walkers, who, unaware of the lily's importance, trample it underfoot. However, it still survives in inaccessible places, and is protected in two National Nature Reserves.

Rough marsh-mallow   *Althaea hirsuta*

The rough marsh-mallow is an annual or biennial herb of the mallow family. It is also known as the 'rough' mallow and the 'hairy' mallow.

Its stalk and leaves are covered with bristly hairs, and its long-stemmed flowers appear from May to July. It is found along the edges of fields and woods, and in dry, grassy places on calcareous soil. In Britain it is considered to be native only to Kent and Somerset, but as a result of its occurrence in crop seed, especially lucerne, it also appears in other parts of the country. It is found in Europe, especially in the South, and in Western Asia.

During the 150 years since it was first recorded in Britain it has varied in its numbers, probably because of fluctuations in the weather pattern at germination time.

The scientific name is derived from 'to soften', and even today herbalists recommend extract of marsh-mallow for treating inflammation of the alimentary canal and the urinary and respiratory systems.

Early spider orchid *Ophrys sphegodes*

The early spider orchid is a perennial, standing between three and fourteen inches tall. Its name, as well as denoting the resemblance of its flowers to spiders, also records the fact that it flowers from April to June. There are generally two or three flowers on each stem, though as many as ten have been recorded. The distinctive H- or X-shaped mark on the lip, which is actually a modified petal, can sometimes look like the Greek letter *pi* (π). The individual flowers are fairly long-lasting.

It occurs on dry banks and grassy places on limestone. It seems to grow well near the coast. It was once quite widespread in Southern England, and was found as far north as Northamptonshire. Now it is confined to some 17 localities south of the Thames – in Dorset, Sussex, Kent, and Gloucestershire. It is still widespread in Western, Central, and Southern Europe.

The species started to decline in Britain about a century ago, long before the destruction of its grassland habitat began. More recently some of its sites have been ploughed up, and human encroachment, especially on the Dorset populations, is a continuing problem. It occurs in one National Nature Reserve, one National Trust property, and six SSSIs. It is classified as vulnerable.

Fen orchid *Liparis loeselii*

The fen orchid is a perennial, standing between two and seven inches tall. At the base of the stem, sheathed in dead leaves, there is a 'pseudobulb' – a swelling that resembles a bulb and serves as a water storage organ. It bears from three to eight flowers which bloom in June and July.

It likes very wet places, such as fens, marshes, and dune slacks, where the water is either alkaline or of neutral acidity. Once found in more than thirty sites in the East Anglian fens and in the dune slacks of South Wales, it is now reduced to just eight sites spread between Devon, Norfolk, Glamorgan, and Carmarthenshire. It is sparsely distributed through Northern, Western, and Central Europe.

It is declining rapidly, with populations at several of the remaining sites numbered in single figures. The main reason for the decline is that its wetland habitat is being drained for conversion into farmland. In East Anglia, where this process is widespread and where even nature reserves give little protection, the species seems unlikely to survive. However, it occurs in three National Nature Reserves and other protected areas. It is endangered in Britain and vulnerable in Europe.

Ghost orchid   *Epipogium aphyllum*

The ghost orchid is a saprophyte, which means that it obtains its nourishment from dead organic matter; it therefore has no leaves and no chlorophyll. It is sometimes called the 'spurred', or 'spur-lipped', coralroot, which is slightly confusing as it is not in the same genus as the coralroot, though both are saprophytes. The established common name, 'ghost orchid', well describes its pale flowers and translucent stem, and indeed its peculiar life cycle.

It is quite small, reaching a height of two to seven inches. The stem carries from one to five flowers, which appear between May and August. It grows among decaying leaves in the deep shade of oak and beechwoods. The species was first discovered in Britain in 1842, and it is likely that few people have ever seen it since that date.

Flowering seems to be spasmodic, and several years may pass before the orchid reappears at the same site (though it has been reported to have flowered almost annually at one site in recent years). The emergence of a flowering stem usually follows a wet spring. There are generally only one or two plants at a particular site, and seed is rarely produced. The sites themselves may be many miles apart.

It occurs at a few places in the Chiltern Hills of Oxfordshire and Buckinghamshire. It used to occur in Herefordshire and Shropshire, but has not been seen in these two counties for many years. It is found through much of Europe and eastward to the Himalayas, though it is nowhere common.

Although the ghost orchid seems always to have been rare in Britain, it is possible – given the large amount of luck needed to find it – that it may be more abundant than we suppose. This mysterious plant would clearly present a great temptation to any collector who happened to see it, and a marauding slug would have even fewer qualms about attacking it. It does not occur in any nature reserve and is considered one of our most endangered plants.

Lady's-slipper orchid   *Cypripedium calceolus*

◄ The lady's-slipper, the most striking and unmistakable of our British orchids, has two notable characteristics. It is the only member of the fairly widespread *Cypripedium* genus that grows here, and it has the largest flower of any orchid in Britain and Northern Europe.

It grows in limestone areas, and favours shaded woodland. The delicate red and yellow flower, which appears in May and June, has long been prized for its beauty, and therefore has been widely collected. (In the days of the stage-coach country people sold it to travellers.) This plundering of the stock has meant that the 20 locations recorded a century ago were by 1950 reduced to a single site in Yorkshire.

Today only one plant remains. It cannot pollinate itself, so although closely guarded, was considered to be doomed to extinction. However, scientists at Kew have located cultivated plants that are almost certainly of British stock, from which they are planning to produce viable seed through cross-pollination. Then by means of a sophisticated laboratory technique, seedlings will be grown, which in due course will be transplanted to suitable habitats.

In Europe the lady's-slipper is found from Norway to the Alps.

Late spider orchid   *Ophrys fuciflora*

The late spider orchid is a perennial, standing from six to twenty-one inches tall. Like those of its relative the early spider orchid, its flowers are thought to resemble spiders. Orchids of this genus, *Ophrys*, all bear flowers that look like small animals, including bees, wasps, spiders, and flies. The flowers of the late spider orchid are relatively large and may number from two to ten on each stem. They bloom from the end of May to July.

The species is found on chalk downs and at the edges of fields where the vegetation is not too long or too dense. It has probably never existed outside Kent, where in the past it was fairly widely distributed. Now it is rare and is confined to about eleven localities; in some of them it is reasonably abundant, in others there are only one or two plants.

It is also found in Central and Southern Europe, where it can be quite variable in appearance, and several distinct races are recognised.

It has suffered greatly during the past half-century from the destruction of chalk grassland, and from a reduction in grazing, which kept the grass at a suitable height.

It occurs in one National Nature Reserve and two SSSIs and is classified as vulnerable.

Lizard orchid   *Himantoglossum hircinum*

The lizard orchid is one of the larger and more robust European orchids, standing one to two – sometimes up to three – feet tall. The central lobe of the flower's lip is elongated and twisted, and looks something like a small lizard. It blooms from May to July, and there may be as many as 70 flowers on each plant. Equally striking is their pungent smell, like that of a billy goat, which is especially noticeable towards evening.

The lizard orchid grows on woodland edges and paths, in scrub, sand dunes, and grassland, and almost always on chalk or limestone. Its distribution and status is highly erratic. By 1900 it was thought to be near extinction, but it slowly recovered, and then increased and spread rapidly between 1920 and 1940. Since then it has declined again and is now known at only six sites in Southern England, with a total of about 300 flowering plants. The fluctuations are probably due to climatic changes. Kent seems always to have been its stronghold. It is fairly widespread in Southern Europe though it is nowhere common.

It occurs in six SSSIs, and is considerered vulnerable, being especially sought after by collectors.

Military orchid *Orchis militaris*

The military orchid is a perennial ground orchid that can grow to a height of two feet, though in Britain the maximum is more like fifteen inches and it is often even shorter than that. There may be many flowers on each spike, and it is these that give the plant its name. The sepals are folded together to form a hood that looks remarkably like an old military helmet. (Another name for the species is 'soldier' orchid.) The flowers appear in May and June.

The military orchid grows on woodland paths and borders and in scrub, always on chalk. It was once fairly widespread in the Chiltern Hills, where it has been recorded in a number of localities, but it vanished from one place after another until it was thought to be extinct. It was not seen from soon after the First World War until 1947, when it was rediscovered in Buckinghamshire – a lapse of nearly thirty years. The botanist J. E. Lousley, who made the discovery, said it was largely due to luck. 'The excursion was intended as a picnic. But I selected our stopping places on the chalk with some care, and naturally wandered off to see what I could find. To my delight I stumbled on the orchid just coming into flower.'

Lousley counted 39 plants in the new colony, of which 18 were in flower. He also noted that those most in the shade were either not flowering at all or were putting up only small spikes. In 1955 another quite large colony was found in Suffolk, far away from the species' previously known range. The colony probably started from seed blown on the wind from Buckinghamshire.

Many theories have been suggested to explain the decline of the species in Britain. Some natural cause may have been responsible, or, (perhaps more likely), changes in woodland management. The military orchid is now carefully protected at both sites, in Nature Conservation Trust reserves, because it is susceptible to trampling, not to mention collecting. The Suffolk plants may be viewed from a raised walkway. The species is classified as vulnerable. It also occurs across much of Central Europe.

Monkey orchid *Orchis simia*

The monkey orchid is similar to the military orchid, but is more slender and shorter (about five to twelve inches). It also has more delicate flowers, which appear in May, just before those of the military orchid, and which often bear a noticeable resemblance to monkeys.

Unlike those of other British orchids, the flowers on each spike open from top to bottom. The leaves contain coumarin (an aromatic substance that is used in the making of scent), and so can give out a pleasant smell of new-mown hay.

It grows on grassland, open scrub, and the edges of fields, mostly on lime. In the last century it was not particularly rare and was found in the Chiltern Hills and in Surrey and Sussex. Today it is confined to four Chiltern colonies: two in Oxfordshire, two in Berkshire (it was transplanted to one, as a conservation measure), and a recently discovered site in Yorkshire. It is also found in Central and Southern Europe and eastwards to Syria and Turkey.

The species' early decline may have been due to natural causes, but more recently it has been subject to collecting, ploughing, the removal of turf, and excessive grazing by rabbits. It occurs in several nature reserves and is classified as vulnerable.

Plymouth pear *Pyrus cordata*

The Plymouth pear is a hedgerow shrub that grows to about ten to twelve feet. Unlike the ordinary wild pear, *Pyrus pyraster*, and of course the cultivated variety, it always has thorns. Its fruits are round rather than pear-shaped.

It was first discovered growing in hedges near Plymouth, and is now confined to two Devon localities. In the past it was also found in Cornwall, but became extinct there for reasons unknown. The species is also found in Western France, and possibly in Greece and Iran.

It has always been rare, and not much is known about it. It does not face the kind of hazards, such as collecting and trampling, with which smaller and more obviously attractive plants have to contend. However, industrial development did pose a threat in one locality, so that plants had to be removed to a safer site.

The cultivated pear is descended from *Pyrus pyraster*, and was probably introduced here by the Romans. The wild fruit has been described as 'hard and harsh, and even schoolboys would leave it for the birds'.

Cheddar pink *Dianthus gratianopolitanus*

The Cheddar pink is a densely tufted perennial herb with a woody stock. It grows to a height of six to nine inches, and its deep pink flowers appear from May to July. They smell strongly of cloves and are very attractive to butterflies and day-flying hawkmoths.

It grows in sunny places on and near carboniferous limestone cliffs at Cheddar Gorge in Somerset. It seems always to have been confined to this area of the Mendip Hills, but has been recorded as an introduction in some other Southern and Midland counties, and in Northern Ireland. It is also sparsely distributed in West and Central Europe.

The wild plant is just as attractive as the garden pink, and so has long been picked and dug up by gardeners and others. At one time, plants were offered for sale, but seeds are now sold instead.

As many thousands of tourists now visit Cheddar every year it is not surprising that the plant survives only in inaccessible places – where it is still fairly numerous. It grows within two SSSIs and is classified as vulnerable. It is also a rare plant in Europe.

Childling pink *Petroraghia nanteuilii*

The childling pink is an annual with a slightly downy stem, standing anything from four to twenty inches tall. It is very similar to the proliferous pink, *P. pro-lifera*, and in fact was once thought to be of the same species. However, when *P. nanteuilii* was recognised in Britain in 1962, some populations were assigned to the one species and some to the other.

The childling pink grows in sandy and gravelly places, usually near the sea. It has been recorded in two locations in Hampshire, two in Sussex, and in Jersey. It seems to have become extinct in Hampshire some time after 1965, but is still common in Jersey. In Sussex it is considered reasonably secure because although it is attractive and easily accessible, it finishes flowering early in the year before the holiday season starts. It grows in one local Nature Reserve and is classified as endangered.

Norwegian sandwort *Arenaria norvegica*

There are two sub-species of the Norwegian sandwort in Britain: the typical sub-species *A. n. norvegica*, which used to be called the 'Arctic' sandwort, and an endemic British sub-species *A. n. anglica*, called the 'English' sandwort.

The Norwegian variety is a perennial herb of the large pink family that grows as a small tuft about two inches high. It has rather fleshy leaves and large white flowers nearly half an inch across, which appear in June and July. It is found on lime-rich screes and river shingle in Inverness-shire, the Inner Hebrides, West Ross, Sutherland, and Shetland. While fairly sparsely distri-buted, it is reasonably abundant and secure in several places. It occurs in a number of reserves, including seven National Nature Reserves, and is classified as rare.

The English sandwort is much more restricted and is found nowhere else in the world. A winter annual or biennial, with even larger flowers than the Norwegian sandwort, it grows in only a few tracks and depressions on limestone in one small area of Yorkshire. This plant is vulnerable to agricultural activities and recreational pressure. It is found in one SSSI and is classified as endangered.

Teesdale sandwort *Minuartia stricta*

The Teesdale sandwort is a perennial of the pink family that forms small, loose tufts. Its slender, erect stems, about two to three inches tall, bear small white flowers that appear in June and July. Formerly known as the 'bog' sandwort it grows only in two damp gravel patches on a boggy fell in Durham, where several hundred plants are protected within a National Nature Reserve. It is classified as vulnerable. Some years ago it very nearly disappeared altogether.

In the mid-1960s one of the most hard-fought and well-publicised conservation battles that Britain has ever witnessed took place over a plan to build a dam at Cow Green in Upper Teesdale. It was foreseen that the dam would wreck a unique community of tundra plants that had survived almost unchanged for 10,000 years. Unfortunately the scheme went ahead, and much of the area was flooded. However, throughout the construction period the Teesdale sandwort was protected from vehicles which might have run over it, and it survived.

The plant is also found at around 1,500 feet in Central Europe and Arctic regions of Europe, Asia, and North America.

Drooping saxifrage *Saxifraga cernua*

The drooping saxifrage is a perennial herb growing from two to six inches tall. It does not always flower, and even when it does it fails to produce any seed, but reproduces by growing small red 'bulbils' at the base of the leaves. These are bulb-like organs that fall off in the autumn and remain dormant until the following spring, when they grow roots and form new plants. Even in Arctic regions, where it flowers in profusion, it still does not set seed, and reproduces only in this way.

It grows in damp pockets and rocky crevices in the mountains, at heights of 3,000 to 4,000 feet. There are some four colonies known in Britain – in Perthshire, Inverness-shire, and Argyllshire. Most of them number fewer than a hundred plants. It is also found in Arctic regions and in the mountains of Europe, Asia, and North America.

Despite, or perhaps because of, its rarity in Britain it has been subject to collecting by botanists and gardeners for more than a century, and it has been suggested that there may now be more examples in herbariums and gardens than there are in the wild. It occurs in one National Nature Reserve and four SSSIs, and is classified as vulnerable.

Tufted saxifrage *Saxifraga cespitosa*

The tufted saxifrage is a perennial that grows in compact cushions two or three inches high: hence the name 'tufted'. Its leaves are covered with short hairs, and its off-white flower appears in June and July. It grows in exposed places among rocks in the mountains, at altitudes of 2,000 to 3,500 feet, and is known in fourteen localities in Caernarvonshire, Aberdeenshire, Banffshire, Inverness-shire, and Ross. It is also found in Arctic regions of Europe, Asia, and North America.

The British colonies are all very small, often numbering fewer than ten plants. Collecting has certainly caused a decline, and the plant can be considered safe only in the most inaccessible sites. In 1976 the summer drought nearly destroyed the North Wales population. It remains to be seen what effect the dry summer of 1983 may have had.

This species now occurs in only two National Nature Reserves and three SSSIs, and is classified as rare.

The name 'saxifrage' comes from Latin words meaning 'rock' and 'break' and derives from the plant's supposed ability to break rocks in crevices where it grows. An alternative name was 'breakstone'.

Whorled Solomon's-seal   *Polygonatum verticillatum*

The whorled Solomon's-seal is a perennial herb whose leaves grow in groups of three to six, in whorls, or rings, around the stem. It stands from one to nearly three feet tall. Its drooping, bell-shaped flowers appear in June and July and are followed by red berries. It grows in mountain woodland and may now be confined to two localities in Perthshire. It has long been extinct in its former sites in Northumberland and Angus. The reason for this is unkown, but may be due to natural changes in the habitat. It occurs in one SSSI and is endangered.

The species is also found in Europe, where it is quite common in beech-woods, and eastward to the Himalayas.

'Solomon's-seal' is so-called because of the leaf scars on the rooting stem, which are said to resemble a star-shaped document seal (similar to the star of David). The presence of the marks indicated its use to early herbalists – for sealing wounds. Gerard recommended its application to 'any bruise . . . gotten by falls or womens wilfulnesse, in stumbling upon their hasty husbands fists, or such like'. Modern herbalists still use the powdered roots as poultices for bruises.

Alpine sow-thistle *Cicerbita alpina*

The alpine sow-thistle is a perennial herb of the daisy family, standing five or even six feet tall. Its stout, furrowed stem has dense reddish hairs, and its small mauve-blue, dandelion-like flowers appear from July to September. It has also been called the 'blue' or 'alpine blue' sow-thistle.

It grows in moist, grassy places on mountain rocks in Angus and Aberdeenshire. About five colonies are now known, mostly in rather inaccessible places and none with very large populations. It has suffered from collecting and from grazing by red deer. In one Aberdeenshire colony in the 1960s there were some 200 plants but there are now very few. It occurs in several nature reserves and is classified as rare.

The species is quite common in the mountains of Europe, and in Switzerland has been recorded at over 7,000 feet. In Lapland the plant's milky stem used to be eaten raw. It could only be eaten when young, as when the flowers appear the stalk becomes hard and woody. Despite its bitterness, the Laplanders were said to relish it (though some of them told Linnaeus that when they first took to using it as food they found its taste very unpleasant).

Adder's-tongue spearwort *Ranunculus ophioglossifolius*

The adder's-tongue spearwort is an annual herb of the buttercup family, growing to a height of a foot or so. It has had a variety of names, including the 'broad-leaved spearwort' and the 'snaketongue crowfoot'. Its yellow flowers appear from May to August, or for an even longer period.

The species once existed in Dorset, Hampshire, Jersey, and Gloucestershire, but has been extinct for a long time in all but the latter county. Until recently it was thought to occur in just one pond in Gloucestershire; it grows on mud which dries out from July to October but is covered in one or two feet of water for the rest of the year. It faces competition, especially in dry years, from sweet-grass (*Glyceria*), but members of the local Nature Conservation Trust actively manage the site to ensure survival of this rare buttercup, which is classified as endangered.

In the 1970s a plan to site a car-wash near the Reserve met national opposition, and was abandoned. In 1983 a new threat arose with the announcement of a plan to build a housing estate and a road that would run within yards of the pond. Fortunately a second Gloucestershire location is now known to exist.

The species is also found in parts of Europe and Asia.

Spiked speedwell *Veronica spicata*

The spiked speedwell is a perennial found in two forms in Britain. The rarer is the sub-species *V.s. spicata* which grows about six inches high and has flowers of varying shades of blue that appear in July and August.

It is found on dry chalk grassland in the Breckland of East Anglia. It was once fairly widespread, but many of the colonies were destroyed by ploughing or by tree-planting. Classified as vulnerable, it survives in four localities in Suffolk, Norfolk, and Cambridgeshire, some of which contain several hundred shoots. One site occurs in a National Nature Reserve.

The second sub-species, *V.s. hybrida*, is much taller, with stems up to 18 inches high and flowers that are rather less brightly coloured. It is found on limestone cliffs near Bristol, and in Wales, Yorkshire, and Cumbria. The population of this sub-species is quite widespread and has hardly declined over the years because the rocky ledges on which it grows are largely safe from depredation. It is not considered threatened.

Purple spurge *Euphorbia peplis*

The purple spurge is an annual herb with a milky juice in its stem. Its crimson branches lie flat along the ground and its greenish flowers appear from July to September. Most euphorbias are tropical, and the foreign species include trees and shrubs. The purple spurge is monoecious, which means that it has both male and female flowers on the same plant. This is generally a useful mechanism for survival, as it needs only one plant to seed itself in a new habitat for the species to become established. Unfortunately it does not seem to have helped the purple spurge to maintain itself in Britain.

It is found on sandy and shingly beaches, and at one time occurred in Cornwall, Devon, Somerset, Dorset, Kent, Cardiganshire, the Scilly Isles, the Isle of Wight, and Lundy Island. It is now probably extinct in all of these places due in some (possibly all) cases to destruction of its habitat by natural causes. Trampling by visitors has been a contributory factor on some beaches.

The plant has occurred recently on two of the Channel Islands, but can be seen regularly only on Alderney. It is classified as endangered.

It is found on the Atlantic shores of Europe and in the Mediterranean.

Starfruit   *Damasonium alisma*

The starfruit is an annual aquatic herb of the water-plantain family. Its name comes from the distinctive star-like form of its fruit. An older name is 'thrumwort'. Its leaves may float on the surface or are sometimes submerged, and its small white flowers appear from June to September.

This species grows on the muddy edges of gravelly ditches and ponds. Populations can vary from year to year as it is dependent on the water-level falling in early summer.

It was once found in more than fifty localities, mostly in Southern England but also in the Midlands and Yorkshire. It has, however, been declining sharply for many years and is now approaching extinction. Since 1970 there have been reliable records from a single locality in Surrey and two sites in Buckinghamshire, though happily there was a report of its rediscovery in Sussex in the summer of 1983. The problem is habitat destruction caused by the filling in, draining, and pollution of ponds.

The starfruit occurs in one SSSI and is classified as seriously endangered.

The species is also found in Western and Southern Europe and North Africa.

Fen violet *Viola persicifolia*

The fen violet is a perennial herb that generally stands around six inches high but occasionally reaches ten inches. It can spread by creeping underground and sending up stems at intervals from buds along the roots. Its flowers appear in May and June.

In Britain it grows in fenland; in Ireland it occurs in damp grassy hollows on limestone. It was formerly found in about 18 separate localities in Suffolk, Norfolk, Cambridgeshire, Nottinghamshire, and Yorkshire, but has disappeared from all of them, apparently because of land drainage. It was also found in Oxfordshire, but in this case it has been lost because of hybridisation with the related heath dog violet. It sur-vives at one location in Huntingdonshire, where in 1972 some 50 plants were reported. By 1975 there were thousands of plants at the same site, mainly on newly disturbed peat, but also on mown rides. It seems to be dependent on such disturbance. In addition, many plants reappeared in 1982 on a nature reserve in Cambridgeshire.

The fen violet now occurs in one National Nature Reserve and one National Trust property. It is classified as endangered.

It is also found in North and Central Europe, and eastward to Central Asia.

Ribbon-leaved water-plantain   *Alisma gramineum*

The ribbon-leaved water-plantain is a perennial aquatic herb that is generally submerged, with few or no leaves above the surface.

The water-plantain family bears a number of striking similarities, both in structure and in appearance, to the buttercup family, and may be derived from it. The small, yellow flowers can be seen from June to September, their petals lasting for only a few hours.

The Dutch botanist H. D. Schotsman studied three closely-related water-plantain species, all of which occur in Britain. He discovered that the flowers of each one open at a different time of day: the ribbon-leaved first, at around 6.15 am; the narrow-leaved species next, at about 9 am; and the common water-plantain four hours later, at 1 pm. It is therefore possible to identify each species by the time of day at which its flowers open.

The ribbon-leaved species has been recorded in Norfolk, Cambridge, and Lincolnshire, but is now extinct in those counties due to dredging of rivers and dykes. Only six plants survive, on the shores of a lake in Worcestershire.

Its range covers Northern and Central Europe and there is strong evidence that the species came to Britain as seed carried on the feet of wildfowl migrating from countries bordering the Baltic. In Britain it occurs in one SSSI and is classified as endangered.

Starved wood-sedge *Carex depauperata*

The starved wood-sedge is a creeping, grass-like perennial belonging to the large sedge family. It grows in dry woods and hedge banks on chalk and limestone and in Britain is now found at only one site in Somerset. Here in the Mendip Hills, an area famous for wild flowers, perhaps as few as eight plants survive on a bank along a country lane. The species was also found in a similar habitat near Godalming in Surrey, where a single plant persisted for many years until it eventually disappeared in 1972. It was found growing in Anglesey in 1967, and it is possible that some plants may still exist there. A small population was discovered in Ireland in 1973. The species is also found in Europe.

Clearly it is on the edge of its range in this country, having always been rare, but in recent years it has also been a victim of woodland and scrub management. J. E. Lousley wrote in 1969 that the bank in Somerset on which it grows was often trimmed in May, just around the time that it flowered.

It is one of Britain's most endangered species. The Somerset population occurs within an SSSI, but it would take only one senseless act for it to disappear from Britain for ever.

Alpine woodsia *Woodsia alpina*

The alpine woodsia is a small fern with fronds that are seldom more than three inches tall. It is found growing in tufts in rock crevices at altitudes of between 1,900 and 3,000 feet. At least seventeen localities are known in Britain – in Caernarvonshire, Perthshire, Angus, Aberdeenshire, Inverness-shire, Argyllshire, and West Ross. At some of these sites there are good colonies – more than a hundred tufts being reported at one site in Perthshire. It is also found in the Arctic and the high mountains of the North Temperate Zone of Europe and North America.

Heavy collecting in the past was responsible for the reduction of this fern's population, and although it is not such a threat today, there have been outbreaks recently in at least two of the known sites. However, the plant is now fortunately confined to the more inaccessible parts of its range, which gives it *de facto* protection. It also occurs within six National Nature Reserves and three SSSIs and is therefore reasonably secure in Britain, though comparatively rare.

In the past, ferns were believed to have considerable magical powers. Carrying fern seed was thought to give one the gift of invisibility.

Oblong woodsia *Woodsia ilvensis*

The oblong woodsia is a diminutive montane fern. At the onset of winter its fronds, which are bright green in July and August, droop to the ground. It resembles quite closely its relative, the alpine woodsia, shown on the previous page, and grows in the same habitat – rock crevices.

It is known in about five mountain locations in Caernarvonshire, Cumberland and Dumfriesshire, and was recently rediscovered in Angus. In the past it also occurred in Merionethshire, Durham and Westmorland, and possibly in Perthshire and the Inner Hebrides. It is found in various parts of Europe and North America.

In Britain the colonies generally contain between three and twenty plants, though in 1965 one Lake District colony was reported to have over a hundred plants, some of them quite luxuriant. In the past the species suffered a decline because of collecting by fern enthusiasts, and this threat remains.

The oblong woodsia is protected in two National Nature Reserves and three SSSIs, and is classified as vulnerable.

Field wormwood   *Artemisia campestris*

The field wormwood is a perennial herb of the daisy family that varies from seven inches to two feet in height.

Its yellowish flowers, which appear in August and September, have virtually no scent, unlike those of its relatives the ordinary wormwood and the sea wormwood, which are very aromatic.

This species grows in bare, often sandy, places and has been recorded in the past from a number of counties as far afield as Cornwall and Fife. It is now confined to a roadside site and some waste land in Suffolk, and to an area of Norfolk Breckland. One Norfolk population was eliminated by chicken farming, and what remains is vulnerable to grazing by rabbits. The Suffolk population has already been drastically reduced because of building, and the largest remaining colony is on a site, one acre in area, which is scheduled for industrial development. The local council has agreed to lease about a quarter of an acre to the Suffolk Nature Conservation Trust for 99 years at a peppercorn rent. If the field wormwoods should die, the land will revert to the council. The Trust is also required to maintain a four-foot fence around the site.

The species, which occurs in no other reserves, is classified as endangered.

Downy woundwort *Stachys germanica*

The downy woundwort is a biennial or sometimes perennial of the Labiate family, reaching a height of between one and three feet. The whole plant is covered with pale, silky hairs. It flowers from July to September.

It grows on limestone, in rather stony pasture, hedgebanks, and roadside verges. Its appearances are very erratic. One year there may be a flourishing colony, and then it will disappear and not be seen again at the same place for some years. Sometimes it may persist for a number of years in succession. Often its reappearances follow disturbance of the ground or scrub clearance.

It has been recorded in Hampshire, Northamptonshire, and Lincolnshire, but its main stronghold seems to be Oxfordshire, where it survives in two localities. No particular threat has been identified, and because of its unpredictable growth-pattern it is difficult to be sure of its status.

It occurs in one SSSI and is classified as endangered. Outside Britain it is found in Central and Southern Europe, North Africa, and eastward to the Orient.

Limestone woundwort *Stachys alpina*

The limestone woundwort is a perennial of the Labiate family and can grow to more than three feet in height. It is rather similar to the downy woundwort, but less hairy.

This species was discovered in 1897, and it is curious that such a tall and presumably conspicuous plant was not found earlier. The original site was in the Cotswold Hills in Gloucestershire, where the plant continued to flourish in open woodland, hedgebanks, and limestone grassland; at one time there were several sites, but now there is only one. Even this was threatened by the overgrowth of rank grasses and by conifer planting, but it has now become a Nature Conservation Trust Reserve and is more secure.

The limestone woundwort was also known at a site in Denbighshire, which was destroyed by road widening in 1960. However, in 1973, another site was discovered in the same area, and two healthy clumps of the plant were reported.

It is classified as endangered. It also occurs in Central Europe.

Greater yellow-rattle _Rhinanthus serotinus_

The greater yellow-rattle is a fairly robust herb of the figwort family. Its long, slender stem reaches a height of two feet. It is a hemi-parasite – that is, it attaches its roots to the root system of an adjacent grass and derives part of its water and mineral needs from the other plant.

The yellow flowers are larger than those of the ordinary yellow-rattle, _R. minor_, but they share the same distinctive shape, like a hooked, pendulous nose – giving rise to the scientific name _Rhinanthus_, which comes from two Greek words meaning 'nose' and 'flower'.

The species occurs in cornfields and waste land, and (much less often) in meadows and on sandhills. It was once widespread in scattered localities in Scotland and Northern England, but was rarer in Southern England and in Wales. It is now known at about four localities in Surrey, Lincolnshire, and Angus. It is reported to be abundant at one chalk grassland site in Surrey. Though it faces no immediate threat, destruction of its habitat seems to be responsible for its general decline. It occurs in no nature reserves and is classified as endangered. It is also found in parts of Northern Europe.

Fauna

Barbastelle   *Barbastella barbastellus*

The barbastelle is a member of the Vespertilionidae family, as are all the British bats except the two horseshoe species. Smallish in size, it has a wingspan of 9½ to 11 inches. Its upper parts are blackish brown with the tips of the hairs pale yellow or cream, giving it a frosted appearance. Its ears are different from other British bats in that they are squat – almost as broad as long – and joined across the forehead. Very little is known about its behaviour. Its flight, which is generally low and often over water, tends to be heavy and fluttering.

It seems to prefer wooded river valleys, and it roosts in trees and buildings. One of the rarest British species, it is very elusive, especially in summer when it is well dispersed. During the winter, in cold weather, it is sometimes found in caves.

It has been recorded in various parts of England and Wales. One or two are caught every year, but there are now no known colonies. Its decline is probably linked to a reduction in its preferred habitat. It also seems to be declining rapidly in Europe.

Bechstein's bat   *Myotis bechsteinii*

Bechstein's bat is of medium size with a wingspan of 10 to 11¾ inches. Its wings are broad and slightly pointed. Its upper parts are light brown and its under parts greyish-buff to white. It is somewhat similar to natterer's bat, except for its very long ears.

It emerges about twenty minutes after sunset and flies slowly, and generally quite low over the ground, on rather stiff wings. It probably feeds mostly on moths, which it eats in flight.

An elusive forest species, it normally roosts in tree holes, both in summer and winter, though it has also been found in buildings and caves. It prefers primaeval forests and old, unmanaged deciduous woodlands; bones of this species are quite commonly found in archaeological sites dating back 3,500 years, to a time when forests in Britain were much more extensive. It has been recorded in several Western and Central English counties, but is now found, very infrequently, in the Hampshire-Dorset area. It seems to be extremely rare, though it is possible that observers have not looked in the right places. Its decline has certainly been due to the contraction of suitable habitat. It occurs throughout Europe but only in very small numbers.

Brandt's bat *Myotis brandti*

Brandt's bat is small, with a wingspan of 8¼ to 10 inches. Its wings are narrow with almost translucent membranes and its ears are fairly short. Its upper parts are reddish-brown.

This species was recognised as separate from the similar whiskered bat in 1970. Until then both had been regarded as a single species, and scientists are still trying to separate them.

It emerges early in the evening, often at sunset, and probably remains active intermittently throughout the night. It sometimes can be seen during the day. Its flight is of medium speed, and fluttering. It is found in wooded country, roosting in buildings in summer and caves in winter, and feeding on small insects and spiders. Its range is uncertain because of possible confusion with the whiskered bat, but positive records have been made from North Devon to Kent and as far north as Yorkshire. Its status is uncertain, but it is possible that it is slowly declining.

It has been positively recorded from most European countries since its recognition in 1970, and is probably fairly widespread in Central and Western Europe.

Brown long-eared bat *Plecotus auritus*

The brown – sometimes called the common – long-eared bat is small to medium in size, with large oval ears measuring over an inch long (almost the length of its head and body). Its wingspan is 9 to 11¼ inches. Its upper parts are usually yellow-buff or greyish-brown. Until recently there was thought to be only one *Plecotus* species, but in the 1960s the genus was divided into two – brown and grey long-eared.

The brown species generally emerges at night-time, but sometimes comes out about twenty minutes after sunset. Initially its flight lasts for about an hour, and then is intermittent throughout the night. It frequently hovers among trees, where it takes insects off leaves (though it also catches them in the air). It eats small insects in flight, but takes some to a perch to be consumed. In summer, noctuid moths are thought to form its main diet.

It prefers sheltered, lightly-wooded areas and probably occurs throughout Britain except in the exposed parts of North-West Scotland. After the pipistrelle it is our most abundant bat. There is no reliable information about its status, but it is probably declining. It is found in Ireland and across Asia and Europe to Japan.

Daubenton's bat *Myotis daubentonii*

Daubenton's bat is a small species with a wingspan of 9 to 10½ inches. It has short ears and very large feet. Its upper parts are brown, its under parts pale buff-grey. It emerges about thirty minutes after sunset and seems to be active more or less throughout the night. Its flight is steady and fairly fast, and often along regular 'beats'. It has been caught over water, and feeds mainly on small insects which it eats during flight.

It frequents open wooded country where it roosts in hollow trees and buildings. During the summer, adult females form large nursery colonies in buildings, but in winter the species is more dispersed, though several may be found together, sometimes in caves.

The species is widespread in England and Wales, and in Scotland to just north of Inverness. At most roosts in Britain there seems to be a slight decline in numbers, yet at two sites in Suffolk numbers have increased three- or four-fold over the last 20 years.

The species probably occurs throughout Ireland, in most of Europe, and eastward to Japan.

Greater horseshoe bat *Rhinolophus ferrumequinum*

The greater horseshoe bat is one of two British members of the Rhinolophidae family. It is a large bat with big ears and a wingspan of 13½ to 15½ inches. It has a complex series of nose-leaves on its muzzle, part of which form a horseshoe shape.

It emerges about thirty minutes after sunset and is active throughout the night. Its flight is heavy and fluttering and usually quite low over the ground. It mainly catches insects in flight.

It roosts in large roof spaces in barns and other buildings, and in winter hibernates in caves, mines, and cellars.

This species occurs in South-West England and South Wales, and the population is stable at about 2,200: a number which, however, represents a very considerable decline from 250,000 or more in the last century. Many roost sites have been lost, and the species is very vulnerable to disturbance by torch-light and even the slightest noise.

It also occurs in Southern and Central Europe, North Africa, and Asia.

Grey long-eared bat *Plecotus austriacus*

The grey long-eared bat is similar in appearance and behaviour to the brown long-eared bat, but is greyer in colour and slightly bigger. Its ears are very large and broad and its wingspan is 10 to 11¾ inches. It emerges late in the evening and is intermittently active throughout the night.

In Europe it seems to prefer lowland cultivated valleys, with nursery roosts in and around villages and small towns. In Britain the only known colony is in Dorset, under the roof of a house, in open, lightly-wooded country. There may be other colonies, as individuals have been found in Southern Hampshire, Sussex and Devon. Discoveries of specimens at archaeological sites in the North Pennines, the Midlands, and East Anglia prove that in the past the species was more widely distributed. ▶

Its current status is unknown, except that it is obviously very rare.

It also occurs in Central and Southern Europe, North Africa, and eastward to the Himalayas.

Leisler's bat *Nyctalus leisleri*

Leisler's bat is medium-sized with a wingspan of 11 to 13½ inches. Its wings are narrow and pointed and its ears are short. Its upper parts are a dark golden or rufous brown, with the hairs darker at the roots. The under parts are distinctly lighter in colour.

It emerges early in the evening, at or soon after sunset, and is mainly active for two periods of about an hour each just after sunset and before sunrise. It is occasionally active during the day, especially in the autumn. It flies straight and fast, with shallow dives, usually at tree-top level or higher, feeding in flight on medium to large insects. It is essentially a woodland species, roosting in tree holes, but in Britain it also frequents buildings.

Though found in widely scattered areas of Central, and perhaps Southern, England, it is very rare, and in some years, apart from two or three colonies, it may not be recorded at all. It could, however, be on the increase at the expense of the noctule, which has similar habits and which it resembles. It is probably a migratory species.

It has a rather scattered distribution through most of Europe and eastward to the Himalayas. It occurs in Madeira and the Azores, and seems to be quite abundant in Ireland.

Lesser horseshoe bat *Rhinolophus hipposideros*

The lesser horseshoe bat is similar to the greater horseshoe, but is much smaller and more delicate. Its wings are broad and rounded at the tips, spanning 8¾ to 9¾ inches. Its ears are a very distinctive shape. Its upper parts are grey-brown, its under parts paler. It has a distinctive nose-leaf like that of its larger relative.

Emerging about twenty minutes after sunset, it is active throughout the night. Its flight, which is erratic and fluttering, is similar to that of the greater horseshoe, but it has a more rapid wing beat and it glides and turns suddenly. It feeds on a variety of small insects and spiders.

It inhabits mainly wooded country and forms quite large colonies in summer, when it roosts in attics and farm buildings. In winter it is almost always solitary, hibernating in caves, tunnels, and cellars.

It is found mostly in South-Western England, throughout Wales, and as far north as Yorkshire. It has declined by fifty per cent or more in the past twenty years; its food – which seems to be mainly craneflies – is still abundant, so the reason may lie in some other factor, possibly climatic change. It is easily disturbed, so is difficult to study.

It occurs in Western Ireland, Europe, North Africa, and eastward to Kashmir.

Mouse-eared bat *Myotis myotis*

The mouse-eared species is Britain's largest bat, with a wingspan of 14½ to 17½ inches and a weight of up to 1½ ounces. It has large ears and an almost bare face. Its upper parts are medium to light brown and its under parts greyish white, with a distinct demarcation line along the side of the neck. The species did not become established in Britain until well after the Second World War.

It emerges very late and returns while it is still dark. Its flight is slow, heavy, and generally straight, and it feeds mainly on large moths and beetles. It lives in open, lightly-wooded country, roosting in buildings and caves during both summer and winter. In summer, the females gather in large colonies, but in winter they are more dispersed. Males tend to be solitary. Only two colonies have been recorded in Britain. The Dorset colony has become extinct through collecting and disturbance. At the Sussex colony some 70 bats were known to exist until 1974 when they were struck by an unaccounted-for disaster and all the females apparently died. By late 1983 just two males survived.

The species occurs through much of Europe and eastward to Israel, but in North-West Europe it has been greatly persecuted and is extinct over a wide area.

Natterer's bat *Myotis nattereri*

Natterer's bat is a medium-sized species with a wingspan of 10 to 11¾ inches. Its wings are broad but pointed. Its upper parts are light brown, its under parts very light buff or grey, with a clear demarcation line from shoulder to ear. Its ears are fairly long and narrow.

This species emerges soon after sunset and has several periods of activity during the night. The time of its emergence may be related to light intensity and to temperature: when the daytime temperature has been high it comes out later in the evening. Its flight is slowish, and usually around woodland and parks, though sometimes over water. It feeds on small insects, including moths, which are mostly caught in flight but occasionally taken off leaves. It roosts in buildings, hollow trees and caves. Summer colonies may be quite large but in winter it tends to be found singly or in small groups.

Widespread in England and Wales and the southern part of Scotland, it seems to be expanding its range, as there is a recent record from north of Inverness. It is, however, believed to be declining in numbers.

It occurs in Ireland, throughout most of Europe, in North Africa, and eastward to Japan.

Noctule *Nyctalus noctula*

The noctule is a large bat with a wing-span of 12½ to 15¼ inches and a weight of up to 1½ ounces. Its ears are short and its fur a rich golden-brown, the colour reaching right down to the roots.

This species usually emerges about twenty minutes after sunset, though sometimes earlier. It flies high and direct to its feeding area and is then intermittently active throughout the night. Its flight is straight with repeated dives, presumably to catch the larger insects on which it feeds.

It is colonial and roosts in trees, though sometimes also in buildings. A summer roost (which may be in a wood-pecker hole or a hollow tree) can often be identified by noisy squeaking and a dark brown streak of urine or faeces on the trunk. Colonies of up to 1,000 have been found in Europe. Deaths have been recorded after prolonged frost, and some during tree-felling. Starlings may also drive the noctules out of their roost holes, and kill them.

They are found in all woodland habitats, including isolated trees in suburbia. They occur in most of England and Wales, where although their numbers are unknown they are thought to be declining. They are also found across Europe and Asia to Japan, but not in Ireland.

Pipistrelle _Pipistrellus pipistrellus_

The pipistrelle is the commonest and smallest British bat, weighing about a quarter of an ounce or less, and with a wingspan of 7½ to 10 inches. Its wings are fairly narrow and its ears are short and broad.

It emerges about twenty minutes after sunset and is active intermittently throughout the night, sometimes returning to the roost after sunrise. Its flight is fast and jerky, and often quite high up in the sky. It catches mainly small insects which it eats in flight; larger ones are taken to a perch. It flies later in the autumn than most bats and is sometimes seen during the winter. It roosts in quite large colonies of up to several thousand, congregating in buildings and trees and preferring small crevices under roof tiles or cavity walls, where it sometimes sleeps.

It is found throughout Britain in all kinds of habitat except very exposed regions. Most bat records are of this species, yet there appears to have been at least a fifty per cent decline in England since the late 1970s, which may be due to unsuitable weather, or as a result of chemical treatment of buildings to combat woodworm.

The pipistrelle is widespread in Europe, eastward to Central Asia, and in North Africa.

Serotine _Eptesicus serotinus_

The serotine is a large bat with a wingspan of 13½ to 15 inches. It has broad wings, moderately long ears, and conspicuously large teeth. Its upper parts are dark brown, while the under parts are usually paler.

This species generally emerges some twenty minutes after sunset, but the bats that are not roosting in colonies may come out at any time between sunset and complete darkness. It is probably active intermittently throughout the night. When it first emerges its flight may be straight and level but when feeding it dives steeply. It eats mainly beetles and the larger moths.

It prefers lightly-wooded country, but in Britain it roosts mainly in houses and is seldom found in tree holes or caves. In summer the females gather in large nursery colonies, while the males are usually solitary. Its range used to be confined to the South and East, but it now seems to be spreading to West Wales and North Yorkshire. Numbers recorded at most colonies have been decreasing for the last 20 years. A similar pattern of increasing range and decreasing numbers is evident in Northern Europe. It is quite widespread in other parts of Europe, North Africa, and eastward to Korea.

Whiskered bat   *Myotis mystacinus*

The whiskered bat is small, with a wing-span of 8¼ to 9½ inches. It has small feet, relatively long and narrow ears, and a dark coat. Its wings are narrow, with almost transparent membranes.

It emerges early in the evening, usually around sunset, and is probably active intermittently throughout the night. In winter and spring it is also seen quite frequently during the day. Its flight is of medium speed and fluttering, and often along a regular 'beat' over a hedgerow. It feeds on small insects and spiders.

It is found in wooded and open country, roosts in buildings and trees and, in winter, sometimes in caves. It probably occurs throughout England, Scotland and Wales, but seems to be declining slowly; its decline may be greater in Eastern England than in other areas.

It occurs in Ireland, Europe, North Africa and eastward to Japan – though some records may be misidentifications of Brandt's bat.

Otter   *Lutra lutra*

The otter is a carnivore and a member of the weasel family, or Mustelidae. The male is about four feet long, including its one-foot-six-inch tail. It weighs about 23 pounds. The female is smaller.

The otter is a land mammal, but is well adapted for hunting in the water; all its toes are webbed. Although solitary and mostly nocturnal, it may be active in the daytime when undisturbed by man. It usually prefers coarse fish and eels to salmon and trout because they are easier to catch.

The otter lives beside rivers, lakes, marshes, and on the coast. It is scarce or absent in most of England, except in the West Country where an increase in population has been noted recently. It is reasonably plentiful in Mid-Wales. The Highlands and Islands and the North and West coasts of Scotland seem to hold the highest populations in Britain. The species has a huge range, from Ireland to Japan and from the Arctic to North Africa, but its numbers have decreased.

Its decline in Britain began in the late 1950s as a result of contamination from highly toxic pesticides. It has also been affected by the widespread destruction of riverside vegetation and the disturbance caused by human leisure activities.

Red squirrel   *Sciurus vulgaris*

There is a saying that in Saxon times a squirrel could go from the Severn to the Wash without touching the ground. Now, regrettably, most of our forest cover has been lost, and this has been the main cause of the decline in the number of red squirrels. As it prefers extensive stands of mature conifers, the red squirrel thrives mostly where such forests occur – such as Scotland, Wales, and Northern England. It is also found in Brownsea Island, the Isle of Wight, and North Norfolk. Scots pine seeds are its favourite food: one red squirrel can consume as many as 40,000 pine cones in a year.

The grey squirrel was introduced from the United States in 1876, and although it does not appear to compete directly with the red, it has certainly taken over many parts of its range. The number of red squirrels tends to fluctuate from one year to the next, and the grey takes advantage of the red's temporary absence. When this happens the red squirrel seems unable to repossess its former territory.

It is classed as vulnerable rather than endangered, and its future will depend on the existence of large pine woods, which, ironically, conservationists would like to see mixed with deciduous trees.

Bottle-nosed dolphin *Tursiops truncatus*

The bottle-nosed dolphin belongs to the family Delphinidae, which comprises a large number of slender, streamlined cetaceans with beak-like snouts. It can measure up to twelve feet in length, and has a distinct but shortish beak about three inches long. Its back is black, its belly white, and its fin is rather tall and backward pointing.

It feeds mainly inshore on a wide variety of fishes and cuttlefish. It takes salmon in the summer, and has been seen to round them up, forming a holding circle while other dolphins feed beneath the surface.

It is highly intelligent and not afraid of man, and has often befriended swimmers and yachtsmen. Though not as active as the common dolphin, it can leap fifteen feet and is the species most often exhibited in captivity.

It is common in small groups in British waters, mainly around the South and West coasts of Britain and Ireland, and is often seen in estuaries – even the Thames. There has been some decline in the southern North Sea, English Channel and north Irish Sea, probably due to pollution and over-fishing.

The species is widespread throughout the world in all temperate and tropical waters, though seldom in the open sea.

Common dolphin *Delphinus delphis*

The common dolphin is the quintessential dolphin, typical of the Delphinidae family. It is generally about six feet long but may reach eight feet, and has a conspicuous beak about six inches long. It is one of the most brightly-coloured dolphins, with intersecting patches of yellow and white on its flanks. An active and speedy swimmer, it frequently leaps clear of the water, and enjoys 'bow-riding' on the pressure wave in front of boats. It also comes to the aid of wounded group-members, and is said to have done the same for humans.

It feeds on a variety of fish, including mackerel, herring, sprats, and sand eels. When feeding, it often displays frenzied activity, with individuals co-operating to create panic among shoals of fish.

In British waters, this species generally occurs in groups of fewer than 10, though at least 175 were seen in the Bristol Channel in 1972. It is quite often sighted, especially in the South and West and is not rare, though it seems to have suffered in some areas from pollution, disturbance, and over-fishing.

It is a very widespread species, occurring worldwide in all temperate and tropical waters, but it is not found quite as far north as the bottle-nosed dolphin.

Harbour porpoise *Phocoena phocoena*

The harbour, or common, porpoise is a member of the small Phocoenidae family. It is the commonest and smallest cetacean in British waters, generally less than five feet long. Rather stoutly built, it has a short, blunt head with no trace of a beak. Its back, flippers and tail-flukes are black, while its belly is white. The name porpoise comes from the Latin *porcus piscis*, or 'pig fish'.

It is a rather timid species, easily disturbed by noise. It is also a fairly slow swimmer and hardly ever leaps out of the water. It feeds on a variety of fish, such as herring, sole and whiting.

Occurring in schools which average 10 to 15 but can be up to several hundred, it frequents coastal areas and often swims many miles up major rivers. It is most often seen off the coasts of Northern Scotland and South-West Ireland. There has, however, been a marked decline recently in the southern North Sea, the English Channel and the Irish Sea, probably because of pollution, over-exploitation of fish stocks, and, in some areas, an increase in shipping. It is now rarely seen off European coasts where it was once very common, but is widely distributed in the North Atlantic and neighbouring seas, as well as in the North Pacific.

Avocet *Recurvirostra avosetta*

The avocet is an elegant wader with a striking upcurved bill which it sweeps from side to side through the water as it feeds on small invertebrates. Its common and scientific names probably come from the Italian *avocetta,* which in turn is derived from the Latin *avis,* meaning bird.

Its breeding habitat is shallow brackish lagoons near the coast, with low islands and gently sloping banks for feeding: a specialised habitat not very common in Britain. It once bred regularly in Eastern England, but numbers declined in the late eighteenth century, and it ceased breeding altogether in about 1843. The reason is unknown, but in those days both the birds and their eggs were eaten.

It did not begin to breed again here until the early 1940s, when large areas of Eastern England were under wartime restrictions. In 1947 several pairs bred at Minsmere and at Havergate Island in Suffolk. There are now some 150 breeding pairs spread between the two sites, both of which are well protected reserves of the Royal Society for the Protection of Birds. From 15 to 20 pairs breed in other places, and small numbers also visit South-West England in the winter. The avocet population and range may both be increasing slightly in Britain. It is patchily distributed in Europe and Central Asia, and East and South Africa.

Bittern *Botaurus stellaris*

The bittern is a large wading bird which belongs to the same family as the heron. It is skulking and secretive by nature, and seldom flies or ventures into the open. It is heard more often than it is seen: the booming call of the male resembling a ship's foghorn. This territorial call, though not especially loud, can carry over two or three miles.

The bittern is found exclusively in wetlands, where it breeds in large *Phragmites* reed-beds, feeding on fishes, frogs, small birds, and other animals. It was once abundant in Britain, and roast bittern was a favourite country dish, but its numbers were reduced by drainage of fens for conversion into farmland, and by shooting and egg-collecting. By 1868 breeding had ceased. However, nearly fifty years later, in 1911, it began again in Norfolk and gradually increased. It now occurs in several places, its strongholds being in East Anglia and Lancashire, where at its Minsmere and Leighton Moss Reserves the RSPB has created new reed-beds. About half the estimated 40 pairs are in these two reserves, and the others are also in protected sites. There has been a decline in recent years.

It is also found across Europe and Asia to Japan, and in South Africa.

Cirl bunting *Emberiza cirlus*

The cirl bunting is a small, finch-like bird, not unlike the closely-related yellowhammer. It sings from exposed places such as the outer branches of trees and television aerials.

It is mainly seed-eating and lives on farmland in the shelter of hedgerows and trees. It is often found on the lower slopes of downland, generally around villages. It is thought to have first colonised Britain round about 1800, and subsequently became fairly common over the southern half of England and much of Wales, with birds nesting in scattered areas as far north as Yorkshire and Cumberland.

It was at its most abundant around the turn of the century. A gradual decline then set in, and it is now rare. A survey carried out by the British Trust for Ornithology in the summer of 1982 showed that its numbers had dropped by forty per cent in less than ten years, to a maximum of 146 pairs. The vast majority (110 pairs) were in Devon; Somerset was the only other county to reach double figures. This resident bird is very faithful to its home area and is therefore vulnerable to cold winters. Its decline is probably due to gradual climatic change.

It is also found in countries around the Mediterranean.

Snow bunting   *Plectrophenax nivalis*

The snow bunting breeds farther north than any other song bird. Its name no doubt comes from the handsome black and white summer plumage of the male. The female is clothed in a much duller garb of sandy browns.

Fair-sized flocks of snow buntings visit Britain in the winter, feeding quietly along Scottish and English coasts and on some inland Scottish hills. There seem to be two races breeding in Britain, one originating in Scandinavia and Greenland, the other from Iceland. In summer they breed only on the highest mountains of Scotland, such as the Cairngorms.

They were first proved to be breeding in Scotland in 1886, and have since caught the imagination of ornithologists – and unfortunately of egg-collectors as well. Numbers seem to fluctuate over the years: the species is on the southern edge of its breeding range, and the incidence of birds nesting in Scotland has been correlated with the severity of winters in Scandinavia and Iceland.

Though the current population is fewer than 10 pairs, little conservation action is possible, apart from keeping the location of nests secret.

The species has a circumpolar distribution in the Arctic.

Honey buzzard 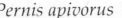 *Pernis apivorus*

The honey buzzard is a large bird of prey rather similar in appearance to the buzzard, *Buteo buteo*. Its plumage is very variable, like that of other buzzards, and is not much help in identification.

In flight it glides with slightly drooping wings (the ordinary buzzard holds its wings in a shallow V), and its display flight is butterfly-like, with the wings flapping overhead. It spends much less time in the air than most birds of prey.

It prefers a mixture of mature deciduous woodland and open spaces, hunting on the ground and eating small mammals, young birds, eggs, the larvae of wasps and bees, and especially honey – hence its name. In fact the arrival of honey buzzards in Britain, and thus their breeding cycle, seems to be timed to coincide with the maximum abundance of wasp and bee larvae.

The species has probably never been very numerous in this country. Nevertheless, like other birds of prey it was heavily persecuted in the eighteenth and nineteenth centuries, as well as being subject to the depredations of collectors. From a rough estimate it would appear that some 15 pairs now exist in four areas of Britain – the most important one being the New Forest.

It is also found in Eurasia and Indonesia.

Chough *Pyrrhocorax pyrrhocorax*

The chough is a medium-sized black crow, easily distinguished from other members of its family by its bright red bill and legs. Its name is probably onomatopaeic, reflecting its call, and ought to be pronounced 'chow' rather than 'chuff'.

It is found among steep coastal cliffs and in mountains, where it nests on ledges or in crevices, often in caves, and occasionally in quarries and old mines.

It was once quite widespread in Britain. The coat of arms of Thomas à Becket, which featured three choughs, is commemorated in the arms of the city of Canterbury. And in *King Lear* Shakespeare had them 'wing the midway air' at the cliffs of Dover. They were also common in Cornwall. In the past, along with other crows, they were subject to maltreatment by humans, especially in the Highlands of Scotland. In South-West England, however, they were protected by superstition: country people believing that the spirit of King Arthur lived on in the form of a chough.

Now they are confined to the coast of Wales, the Snowdon area, the Isle of Man, and the Scottish islands of Islay and Jura. After a long decline the population appears to be fairly stable at about 1,000 pairs.

It also occurs in Europe, and eastward to the mountains of Central Asia. It is quite abundant around the Irish coast, especially in the West and South.

Corncrake *Crex crex*

The corncrake is an elusive rail that likes to remain hidden among thick cover; it is therefore rarely seen, and is best located by its characteristic harsh 'crek-crek' call, which is heard throughout summer nights. The present common name is misleading, as the corncrake frequents grassy meadows and hayfields rather than cornfields. The old name of 'hay crake' is more accurate.

It arrives in Britain from its winter quarters in Southern Africa in April and May and nests in grassland. Unfortunately it has been greatly affected by the mechanisation of grass-cutting: nowadays the grass is cut closer to the ground and also earlier in the year. Other factors have been the conversion from hay to silage and the general disappearance of rough, marginal habitats.

The species used to be common and widespread in Britain, and at the turn of the century its evocative call was regularly heard even in the London suburbs of Tooting and Streatham. Now it is found only in the Hebrides, Orkney, and few places on the west coast of Scotland; some forty per cent of the British population is in the Outer Hebrides.

It also occurs in Ireland and across Europe to Central Asia, but is on the decline everywhere.

Spotted crake *Porzana porzana*

The spotted crake is an extremely secretive bird that is very seldom seen or even heard. It tends to be active at dusk and at night, creeping among tangled sedges and other aquatic vegetation at the edges of lakes, rivers and fens. It is reluctant to fly, and about the only way to locate it is to listen for its reiterated 'h'wit, h'wit' call, which has been likened to the cracking of a whip.

It may once have bred quite widely in Britain, but at scattered locations: there have been records from the North of Scotland to the South of England, and from Wales to East Anglia. It could still occur in very small numbers wherever its swampy, fenland habitat remains, but it is unlikely that more than 10 pairs breed in any one year.

As they are such exceptionally difficult birds to locate, their true numbers can only be guessed at. Writing in 1948 about the Norfolk Broads, John Buxton suggested that they might not be as rare as was thought, but were simply 'impossible little brutes to see'.

The decline of the species probably began with the drainage of its fenland haunts in the eighteenth and nineteenth centuries.

The species also occurs throughout Europe and as far as Central Siberia.

Scottish crossbill *Loxia scotica*

There are two principal crossbill species found in Britain – the common crossbill, *Loxia curvirostra*, and the Scottish crossbill, *Loxia scotica*. Two others, the parrot and white-winged crossbills, sometimes occur as rare vagrants. All are rather similar in appearance and all are protected under the Wildlife and Countryside Act. The Scottish crossbill is a stoutly-built finch with very distinctive crossed mandibles. Until recently it was considered to be a sub-species of the common crossbill but is now regarded as a species in its own right and is therefore the only bird species unique to the British Isles.

The crossed mandibles enable the birds to force open conifer cones to extract the seeds, and the bill of each species is adapted according to its chosen food. The Scottish crossbill, which feeds on Scots pine, has a larger bill than the common crossbill, which feeds mainly on spruce.

The Scottish bird is more or less confined to the old Caledonian forests of the Spey Valley and to new plantations in the region. Numbers fluctuate depending on the extent of the cone crop, but there are probably around 2,000 pairs. The common crossbill is found more widely, from Southern Scotland to Southern England, numbers being increased periodically by birds coming in from Europe. It also occurs across Eurasia and in North America.

Stone curlew   *Burhinus oedicnemus*

The stone curlew is a long-legged, ground-living bird whose call is more like that of the ordinary curlew than is its appearance; this wild, haunting 'coor-lee' is heard at twilight and sometimes well into the early hours of the morning. The bird is difficult to find during the daytime, as it is well camouflaged and likes to lie concealed in areas of cover.

It is found on chalk downs, sandy heaths and shingle, roughly corresponding to the chalk belt that crosses England from Dorset to Norfolk. Much of its preferred habitat has been destroyed or altered by cultivation, afforestation, and the encroachment of scrub caused by the decline in rabbits (due to myxomatosis). However, it has proved fairly adaptable and has also taken to nesting on ploughed land. There are probably at least 200 pairs, of which around 80 are in their stronghold in the East Anglian Breckland.

Marginal downland is still being lost, and the species also suffers at the hands of egg-collectors. Pressure from over-eager birdwatchers is a potential problem in some areas.

The stone curlew also breeds in areas from the Baltic to the Sahara and eastward to India and Burma.

Black-throated diver *Gavia arctica*

The black-throated diver is a fairly large aquatic bird which dives from the surface and catches fish underwater by out-swimming them. Its body is streamlined for speed, and its legs are set back to give maximum thrust. However, it pays the price for aquatic agility by being awkward on land, seldom leaving the water except to breed.

Black-throated divers are summer visitors to large freshwater lochs in the Highlands and Islands of North-West Scotland. They need long stretches of water in order to take-off before becoming airborne, and they nest on islands a few feet from the water's edge to avoid predators such as foxes. In winter they move to coastal waters.

Because of their specialised habitat they are vulnerable to fluctuations in water level. If the water rises too much the nests are flooded and if it falls too much they becomed marooned on dry land, and without the protection of water are vulnerable to predators. They are also vulnerable to unintentional disturbance by fishermen, picnickers, and birdwatchers. Probably fewer than 100 pairs breed each summer.

They occur across Eurasia, and in North America where they are called 'Arctic loons'.

Red-throated diver *Gavia stellata*

The red-throated diver is smaller than the black-throated species but has a rather similar appearance and way of life. A notable difference is that it can take off over a much shorter distance, so it frequents the smaller peat lochs. It obtains its food by flying to the sea or to the larger sea lochs.

The peat lochs, or *dubh-lochans*, where many red-throated divers nest, are so tiny that they may not be marked on even the largest-scale maps. They occur in large areas of blanket bog or moorland and are invisible from all but a short distance. Red-throated divers are thus more difficult to find than black-throated. They nest on islands or on the shore, often creating a kind of slipway as they waddle to and from the water.

They breed in North and West Scotland, and – unlike the black-throated – in Orkney and Shetland, where there are smaller lochs and pools. They also have to contend with water level fluctuations and accidental disturbance.

There are about 600 pairs in Shetland alone, and perhaps some 1,500 pairs altogether. The population seems stable. In winter they may be found virtually all around the coastline of Britain and Ireland. They also have a more or less circumpolar distribution.

Dotterel *Charadrius morinellus*

The dotterel is a northern plover notable for its very handsome summer plumage of chestnut, grey and white. In winter it is very much paler. It is remarkably tame and trusting, and from earliest times was considered stupid because it was so easy to catch – often ending up as a plump delicacy at mediaeval banquets. The name dotterel has a similar origin to the word 'dotty'.

It frequents desolate, high mountain plateaus, living amid the short grass, lichens, and moss. It is an unusual species in that in courtship and mating the female is the dominant partner. After egg-laying she goes off with other females, leaving the male to incubate the eggs and tend the young: a classic case of role reversal.

Once quite widespread in Britain, its decline was due to several factors: shooting (both for food and for pure sport); the popularity of its feathers with fly fishermen; and the activities of egg-collectors and trophy-hunters.

Its main stronghold is now in the high Scottish mountains, but it has been found recently in the Scottish Borders and in North Wales. About 60 to 80 pairs breed each year. The chief threat to which it is subject is tourist development in the Highlands, which includes the construction of roads and ski-lifts.

The dotterel also occurs in Europe and Northern Asia, usually in high mountains.

Golden eagle *Aquila chrysaetos*

The golden eagle is a majestic bird of prey which soars effortlessly, sometimes for hours at a time, on broad and powerful wings with their tips splayed out like fingers.

It inhabits rugged mountains and moorlands, occupying a huge territory of 5,000 to 15,000 acres. It builds its substantial nest on a crag or in a tree, usually with an extensive view of the surroundings.

It was once found in the mountains of Wales, England, and Ireland, but is now restricted to the Scottish Highlands and Islands, a few other isolated sites in Scotland, and, since 1969, the English Lake District. Numbers appear to be stable at over 400 pairs, which represents some twenty per cent of the European population.

The species was once heavily persecuted by sheep farmers and gamekeepers, and in less enlightened areas the killing still continues. The use of persistent pesticides in sheep dip in the 1960s also took its toll. In some areas the increase in tourism has brought problems, as has the loss of hunting territory in Southern Scotland through afforestation. But there is a growing pro-eagle lobby in the Highlands.

It also occurs throughout much of the Northern Hemisphere.

White-tailed eagle *Haliaeetus albicilla*

The white-tailed eagle is a mainly maritime species sometimes known as the sea eagle. It is slightly heavier and larger than the golden eagle, and is distinguished by its white, wedge-shaped tail. (The bird in this photograph is a juvenile, whose beak is not fully grown and whose head is a darker brown than that of adults.) It inhabits rocky coasts, and feeds on a wide variety of mammals, birds, and fish. It is also a scavenger.

Once found in Scotland, Ireland, and Wales—and sometimes even in England, it was relentlessly persecuted by shepherds and then by gamekeepers.

Depredations were continued by egg-collectors and trophy-hunters, and the last nest was recorded in Skye in 1916.

Now the species is being reintroduced by the Nature Conservancy Council in co-operation with the RSPB. Since 1975, 52 young eagles have been brought from Norway and released on the Rhum National Nature Reserve in the Scottish Highlands. About two-thirds of them are still thriving.

The white-tailed eagle is found in Europe, where it probably numbers fewer than 1,000 pairs, and in Asia.

Fieldfare   *Turdus pilaris*

The fieldfare is a large, rather gregarious thrush that is sometimes mistaken for a mistle thrush but can readily be identified by its grey head and rump, separated by a saddle of chestnut on its back and wings. It is a noisy bird which in winter gathers in large flocks – often in company with redwings – and can be seen in hedgerows, farmland, grassland, and other open country. Many thousands winter here regularly, moving from place to place in search of food: in Anglo-Saxon, *felde-fare* meant 'traveller across the fields'.

For more than a century the fieldfare has been expanding its breeding range westwards across Europe, eventually reaching Britain where the first ones bred, in Orkney, in 1967. Since then it has nested regularly in small numbers in scattered locations, mostly in Northern England and in Scotland. Those birds which stay to breed in Britain seem to come from Scandinavia rather than from Central Europe, and have been recorded in a variety of habitats, including moorland scrub, wooded hills, forestry plantations, and farmland. The breeding population appears to be static.

The fieldfare is also found across a wide area of Northern Europe and Asia.

Firecrest *Regulus ignicapillus*

The firecrest shares with the more abundant goldcrest the distinction of being Britain's smallest bird. The two are very similar, but the crown of the male firecrest, which it raises and spreads in courtship, is a brighter colour. The firecrest also has a distinctive eye-stripe, and thin stripes leading from its bill which look like a moustache. It is a very active little bird, flitting busily among the foliage in search of insects. Passage migrants are seen along the South Coast in the autumn, in fairly small numbers. Some remain during the winter.

Like the fieldfare, the firecrest has been expanding its breeding range in Europe in recent years. The first proven record in Britain was in the New Forest in 1962, and since then it has bred at a number of places in Southern England. It seems to prefer Norway spruce, but has been found among a wide range of conifers and mixed woodland.

The breeding population is small, probably fewer than 100 pairs, but seems to be increasing; as the bird is difficult to find, there is no precise information. The firecrests that breed in Britain are migratory, but it is not known whether they actually leave the country.

The species is also found in Western Europe, North Africa, and Turkey. A very similar species in North America is called the 'golden-crowned kinglet'.

Garganey *Anas querquedula*

The garganey is the smallest British duck, apart from the teal, and is the only one of our wildfowl that is purely a summer visitor, arriving from its winter quarters south of the Sahara in March and leaving again in September. It is rather similar to the teal, but the male has a distinctive white eye-stripe in place of the teal's broad green stripe. Its pale blue inner wing can be seen in flight. Its name is Italian in origin, as listed by the Swiss naturalist Konrad Gesner in his *Historium Animalium*, published in 1555.

It is a dabbling duck, taking its food of invertebrates and vegetable matter from near the surface of the water by up-ending. It breeds in shallow, and sometimes brackish, freshwater lakes and ponds with plenty of reeds and other vegetation around their edges. Its main stronghold is probably the East Anglian fens, but it has been found in various parts of England and occasionally in Wales and Scotland. Britain is on the edge of its range, and numbers fluctuate but are never very great: there are probably between 10 and 50 pairs each year. Its future will depend on the existence of suitable wetland habitat. It also occurs across the temperate zones of Europe and Asia to the Pacific.

Black-tailed godwit *Limosa limosa*

The black-tailed godwit is a fairly large long-legged wader which in general shape is rather similar to the curlew but has a straight or even slightly upturned bill. The black, as opposed to barred, tail, and prominent white wing-bars, distinguish it from its relative the bar-tailed godwit.

They prefer to breed in damp meadows which are flooded in winter and grazed by livestock in spring. Though they were quite widespread in the past, a combination of land drainage, shooting, and egg-collecting resulted in their disappearance as a regular breeding species by the 1830s. Then four pairs bred in the Ouse Washes in 1953, followed by increasing numbers in succeeding years. The location was not revealed until 1969, by which time the land was safely in the hands of the RSPB, the Wildfowl Trust, and the Cambridge and Isle of Ely Naturalists' Trust. This area still holds about three-quarters of the population, though they do nest in scattered locations elsewhere, including the Somerset Levels. They also occur as passage migrants, and fairly large numbers winter along the South Coast. Outside Britain they are found across the temperate zones of Europe and Asia.

129

Goldeneye   *Bucephala clangula*

The goldeneye is a diving sea duck which is quite easily recognised by its domed and puffy, almost triangular, head. The male bird also has distinctive white spots between its eye and bill. The domed skull contains large air sinuses, which may enable the goldeneye to make its prolonged dives. It generally prefers to nest in tree holes, near lakes and rivers in thickly forested country. The nests are often more than 30 feet above the ground: the young birds simply scramble out and drop to the ground.

This species is a recent colonist in Britain, having first bred in 1970 in the Inverness-shire area – where it has continued to breed – and occasionally in other places. Unfortunately there is a lack of trees with suitable holes, but conservationists, notably the RSPB, have solved the problem by providing many nesting boxes, which the birds take to quite readily. About 50 pairs now breed in Britain and numbers seem to be gradually increasing.

The species also visits Britain in fairly large numbers in winter, mostly frequenting estuaries and coasts but often inland lakes and reservoirs as well. It also occurs across the forest zones of Eurasia and North America.

Goshawk *Accipiter gentilis*

The goshawk is similar to the sparrow-hawk, but larger. Its name derives from the Old English *gos*, or goose, though such a bird would be rather big prey even for the female goshawk. It was, and still is, a species prized by falconers, and in the Middle Ages was reserved for the squirearchy.

It frequents large areas of woodland, especially pine and beech, though its habitat requirements are not stringent. It takes a variety of prey, generally flying low, very swiftly, and with great agility through the trees. It is therefore seldom seen, except when it makes its soaring territorial flights in the spring. It ceased breeding in Britain in the last century – probably because of persecu-tion by gamekeepers – and thereafter only bred sporadically until 1968. There are now some 60 to 70 pairs, mostly in the Highlands and Scottish Borders, but also in the English Midlands. Most, if not all, of these originated from falconers' birds that were lost or deliberately released. Numbers seem to be increasing, despite continued and widespread persecution. Gamekeepers regard the goshawk as vermin as it sometimes takes game-birds. But a bigger threat is from people on the fringes of falconry who steal eggs and nestlings for eventual sale.

The species also occurs across Eurasia and North America, but is declining in Europe.

Black-necked grebe *Podiceps nigricollis*

The black-necked grebe is well adapted to aquatic life, like the divers, but has a longer neck and more squat appearance. In summer its black neck identifies it from other grebes, and its golden ear-tufts gave rise to the alternative name of 'eared' grebe, by which it is also known in North America. It is a capable diver, but prefers to catch insects and other small animals on the surface of water or on vegetation. Its courtship involves a 'dance', in which the birds rear up out of the water, breast to breast or side by side.

It prefers shallow pools with vegetation plentiful on their banks or floating or half-submerged in the water; there is often little open water in such pools. Suitable sites are not common in Britain, and it did not breed here until the early 1900s. It has become more frequent in later years, as part of a general north-westerly expansion of its range in Europe. (Its range has also expanded northwards in North America.) In Britain, numbers are still small, however, with fewer than 20 pairs breeding at about four sites mainly in the Eastern Lowlands of Scotland. It is not subject to much disturbance.

It also occurs in Europe and Asia, as well as in North America.

Slavonian grebe   *Podiceps auritus*

The Slavonian grebe is a brightly-col-oured species that is distinguished from the black-necked grebe by its chestnut neck and its more pronounced ear-tufts, which sweep back to form prominent horns. Its earlier name was 'horned' grebe, which is what it is called in North America. It catches mainly fish and aquatic insects by diving.

It frequents large shallow freshwater lochs with less dense vegetation and more open water than those favoured by the black-necked grebe. It is a colo-nial species, and its nests – which are anchored to emergent vegetation – may be quite close together; also quite close to nests of the black-headed gull.

The first nest was found in Inverness-shire in 1908, and this site is still the nucleus of the breeding population, which has grown to about 60 to 70 pairs. Numbers are increasing slowly and there is speculation that immigration from Iceland or Scandinavia may be continuing. It is vulnerable to human disturbance and the activities of egg-collectors, and can be seriously affected by fluctuations in water level, in the same way as the divers. It winters in small numbers in coastal waters and is also found across Northern Europe, Asia, and North America.

Greenshank *Tringa nebularia*

The greenshank is an elegant long-legged wader which is rather larger and paler than its close relative the redshank, and which is easily identified by its green legs. This is a northern bird on the southern edge of its breeding range in Britain. It can be found in a variety of habitats, from boggy moorland slopes to open pine forest, where it nests on the ground, preferably next to a piece of dead wood or a large stone. When it is sitting, its mottled plumage provides such excellent camouflage that its nest is more difficult to locate than that of almost any other British bird.

It occupies a very large territory, generally around 500 acres, though sometimes there may be only one pair per 7,000 acres. It breeds widely in the Highlands, the Outer Hebrides, and in Orkney and the Shetland Islands numbering perhaps 900 pairs. At present the population seems to be stable. In the nineteenth and early twentieth centuries, collectors sought out its eggs with great determination, but in spite of this, the greenshank's numbers increased.

It is a common passage migrant, with some birds wintering around the coasts of South-West England, and is also found across Northern Europe and Asia.

Mediterranean gull *Larus melanocephalus*

The Mediterranean gull in winter (as in this photograph) somewhat resembles the common gull and in summer the black-headed gull. Immatures are more difficult to identify than adults.

It spends the winter at sea, though on coastal waters. In summer it can be found in salty lagoons and coastal marshes. It is a colonial nester, sometimes in company with other gulls; in Britain it has nested among large black-headed gull colonies, and there have been hybrids between the two species.

As its name implies, this gull's range is restricted mainly to the (Eastern) Mediterranean. Until the 1950s it was known to breed in Greece, Turkey, the northern and western shores of the Black Sea and Hungary. It has since been recorded as breeding in several Northern European countries, and this expansion of its range has led to an increase in the number (now around a hundred) of winter visitors to Britain, mostly to the coasts of Southern and Eastern England. It first bred in this country in 1968, and nests in one or two sites (which happen to be nature reserves). Numbers, however, are very small – with no more than four pairs in most years – and it is clear that there has not been any increase in the initial population.

Hen harrier *Circus cyaneus*

The hen harrier is a handsome bird of prey, with the males (which are grey) and the females (brown) so different in appearance that they were once thought to be separate species.

The hen harrier was at one time quite numerous and widespread, and probably derived its name from its practice of preying on domestic poultry. Like other birds of prey it declined through persecution by gamekeepers and the activities of egg-collectors. By the beginning of the twentieth century it was more or less confined to Orkney and the Outer Hebrides, where because sporting interests were negligible it was not subject to harassment by keepers. It has spread southwards since then into mainland Scotland, North-West England, the Isle of Man, and North Wales. There are now probably more than 450 breeding pairs.

They frequent open moorland and heather-covered hillsides, and have in part been helped by afforestation. In their early stages these wooded areas offer good breeding and hunting habitat, but as the trees mature, the habitat becomes unsuitable. The birds are still heavily persecuted by keepers, although research has shown that their killing of red grouse chicks has little effect on grouse numbers.

The species is found across Europe, Asia, and North America, where it is called the northern harrier or marsh hawk.

Marsh harrier *Circus aeruginosus*

The marsh harrier is a powerful bird of prey that is usually rather inconspicuous as it flaps and glides over its marshland habitat. Its springtime courtship flights are far from inconspicuous, however, involving a spectacular display of high dives and somersaults.

It breeds among large *Phragmites* reed beds, and sometimes one male may support two females in a single marsh. Though once quite common in Britain, the species steadily declined through persecution by gamekeepers, trophy-hunters and egg-collectors, and destruction of its habitat. In the nineteenth century it no longer bred in England, but in 1911 it returned to East Anglia and has managed to hold on since then, despite being almost wiped out by pesticides in the 1960s. Very recently it has staged a dramatic increase and in 1983 some 70 young were raised from 23 nests – all of them in protected areas. Continuing threats are disturbances by visitors on the Norfolk Broads, destruction of potential nest sites, and the illicit use of poisoned eggs or bait. But plenty of suitable habitat remains, so it is hoped that the increase will continue.

The species is also found in North Africa, Europe, and through much of Asia.

Montagu's harrier *Circus pygargus*

Montagu's harrier is very similar to the hen harrier, though more lightly built. It was not recorded as a separate species until the Devon naturalist Colonel George Montagu cleared up the confusion in 1802 – hence its name. It is a summer visitor to Britain, arriving here in April and leaving in September.

It sometimes breeds in similar areas to the hen and marsh harriers, but generally nests in drier habitats. It declined in the nineteenth century like other large birds of prey, and by the beginning of the First World War only a few pairs survived. It then staged a recovery and by the mid-1950s reached 40 to 50 pairs, largely in South-West England. A further decline followed, and from 1975 breeding was only sporadic.

There has recently been a renewal of activity, with six nests recorded in 1983, but unfortunately they are among crops on arable land; such crops may be sprayed, and can be ready for harvesting before the young are able to fly from their nests. To combat the problem, successful wardening schemes have been mounted by the RSPB with the co-operation and goodwill of local farmers. A further hazard remains, which is disturbance by too many bird-watchers.

The species is also found in North Africa, Europe (where it faces the same problems as in Britain) and into Asia.

Hobby   *Falco subbuteo*

The hobby is a supremely agile and speedy falcon, smaller than the peregrine, whose displays of aerial skill are a delight to watch. It feeds on insects, such as grasshoppers and dragonflies, and small birds, especially swallows, martins and swifts. It is a summer visitor from south of the Sahara, arriving and departing with the birds on which it preys. Its name may come from the old French *hober*, 'to stir', perhaps because it sometimes stirs up flocks of roosting swallows. Its main habitat is downland or heath, with clumps of trees for nesting.

It was once the least studied British bird of prey, but recent observations suggest that it may frequent a much greater variety of habitats. There are some 400 to 500 breeding pairs, mostly in Southern England, and numbers may be increasing.

In Britain it seldom preys on seed-eating birds, except skylarks, so is less exposed to toxic chemicals than some species. Nor does it take game-birds, so it is not much persecuted by keepers. Its eggs have always attracted collectors, but it will often lay a second time.

It is also found in North Africa, Europe, and across Asia to the Pacific.

Hoopoe   *Upupa epops*

The hoopoe is one of the most distinctive and conspicuous birds found in Britain. Larger than a mistle thrush, it has cinnamon-coloured plumage with boldly barred black and white wings and a black-and-white-tipped crest. Its name is derived from its distinctive call – a deep, far-carrying, 'hoo-hoo-hoo', or according to some listeners 'poo-poo-poo'.

It frequents various kinds of open and wooded country, but in Britain is most often seen in large gardens and parkland. It nests in holes in old or rotten trees, or in buildings or walls. As it feeds in the open and is not particularly shy, it is comparatively easy to spot.

It generally winters in Africa south of the Sahara, and those arriving in Britain in the spring are probably migrants that have overshot Spain or France on the journey north. In most years a hundred or more are recorded, generally in Southern England. Though a few may stay on to breed, the species is unlikely to become better established here because of the relative scarcity of its preferred prey of grasshoppers, crickets and small lizards.

It is found widely across Europe and Asia and in much of Africa.

Red kite   *Milvus milvus*

The red kite is the only large bird of prey with a sharply forked tail that is likely to be found in Britain. It has a light, buoyant flight and can sometimes be seen hovering motionless on the wind or gliding across hillsides.

Once one of the commonest and most familiar British birds, it was during the Middle Ages a valued scavenger, keeping the streets clear of carrion and other unpleasant refuse. But with the improvement in public hygiene there was less for kites to eat, and they began to disappear. Like other birds of prey, they then became subject to persecution, and by 1900 there were only a dozen left in the steep, oak-clad valleys of Central Wales.

They are very vulnerable to disturbance: their nests are still robbed of eggs and young, and their habitat is being altered by afforestation of the upland sheep walks. Nevertheless, as a result of dedicated protection by the Welsh 'Kite Committee', numbers have risen to about 40 pairs and are still increasing slowly. Now much cherished by Welsh farmers, this seems to be the one bird of prey that nobody ever has a bad word for. It is also found in Europe and North Africa and eastwards to the Caucasus.

Merlin   *Falco columbarius*

The merlin is a member of the falcon family. Its name could be from *émerillon*, an old French word meaning blackbird – which was considered the largest prey that it was likely to take. It is in fact not much bigger than a blackbird, and is Britain's smallest bird of prey, whose flight is low, fast, and dashing. It hunts small birds such as pipits, larks, buntings and finches (but only the occasional blackbird); also insects and small mammals. In the Middle Ages it was used for hawking by ladies of the nobility.

It generally breeds in high moorland, fells and blanket bogs, where it often nests on sloping ground that affords a good view of the surroundings. It plucks or dismembers its prey on a rocky outcrop, or 'plucking post', near its nest, before passing it to its mate. As the uplands are almost devoid of small birds in the winter, the merlin follows its prey to lower levels, particularly coastal farmland.

It now breeds in the higher areas of Wales, Northern England, and Scotland, and may number 300 to 400 pairs. Since about 1900 there seems to have been a gradual decline. It is widespread in Europe, Asia, and North America.

Golden oriole *Oriolus oriolus*

The golden oriole is a very distinctive woodland bird, but despite its bright gold and black plumage it is surprisingly well camouflaged in its leafy surroundings. Its fluting and rather loud 'weela-weeo' call is heard more often than the bird is seen.

It breeds mainly in mature deciduous or mixed woodland, but sometimes among conifers. In Britain it has nested in large gardens and parks and more recently in large poplar plantations. The nest is made of grasses and is slung like a hammock between the branches of a horizontal fork, generally quite high up.

It seems to have been expanding its breeding range in North-West Europe. It has, for example, increased its numbers in Denmark and has been breeding in Southern Sweden since the 1940s. In Britain it has bred sporadically for a century or more (maybe for much longer) but has done so in greater numbers since the 1950s, and there are now established breeding populations in a few areas of Southern and Eastern England.

It faces no real threats here, though in one locality it is subject to pressure from eager bird-watchers. However, there is so far no evidence that it has suffered from these attentions.

British and European golden orioles winter in tropical East Africa and possibly further eastwards. The species breeds in a broad area of Europe and across to Siberia.

Osprey *Pandion haliaetus*

The osprey is a large fish-eating bird of prey with distinctive white under parts and a small white head. It hunts by plunging – often from 100 feet – talons-first into the water to catch pike, roach, trout, flounder and other fish.

It breeds in Scotland in areas free from human disturbance and close to open water well stocked with fish. Its large nest built of sticks is generally sited on top of conifer trees. Though they were once quite common, in the nineteenth century ospreys were killed indiscriminately, and their further decline was hastened by egg-collectors. By the beginning of the First World War breeding had come to an end altogether; it was not to start again until the 1950s.

In 1959 a pair bred for the first time at Loch Garten on Speyside, and under the watchful eyes of RSPB wardens, ospreys have nested there ever since. They have also started to breed again elsewhere in the Scottish Highlands, and by 1983 thirty pairs were recorded. This slow but perceptible increase seems likely to continue: nest sites are kept secret, apart from those at Loch Garten and the Loch of Lowes, where hides are provided for viewing.

The osprey occurs in many other parts of the world.

Barn owl *Tyto alba*

The barn owl is a ghost-like creature of the night that has long been surrounded by superstition. In earlier times its appearance and its eerie, blood-curdling shriek were associated with evil. 'The owl shriek'd at thy birth – an evil sign', were according to Shakespeare the words with which Henry VI accused his murderer, Richard Crookback.

It inhabits open country and farmland, nesting in barns, ruins, church towers, haystacks, hollow trees, or holes in cliff faces, feeding on small birds and small mammals. Though still widespread in Britain, it has been on the decline recently. It has probably been badly affected by modern farming methods, and is also killed by cars as it flies low over motorways. And it is still shot and trapped. There may now be only 5,000 pairs left – fewer than half the number known to exist in the 1930s – and it is very rare in much of Southern and Eastern England. In most other parts of the world, except in equatorial forests and very cold regions, it is widespread.

▶

Peregrine   *Falco peregrinus*

The peregrine is a fairly large falcon, its long wings and short tail giving it an anchor-like outline in flight. Its hunt is spectacular as it folds back its wings to plummet from a great height in a power dive, or 'stoop', that has been estimated at over 150 mph. It is especially prized by falconers, and in the Middle Ages was protected. The name probably stems from its 'peregrinations', or habit of wandering from the nest when the breeding season is over.

It nests on cliff ledges both inland and on the coast, and is found in Northern Ireland and Western Britain. It was hard hit by pesticides in the 1950s and 1960s but has recovered to about ninety per cent of the pre-1939 level, now numbering some 700 pairs. It has re-colonised most of its former haunts, and some new ones: the rate of recovery being far better inland than at coastal sites, perhaps because of marine pollution. In spite of the Wildlife and Countryside Act, many nests are raided by irresponsible falconers and others, stimulated by the high prices paid for a peregrine – up to £1,000 in Germany and even more in the Middle East.

It occurs in many areas of the world, including all major land masses.

Red-necked phalarope *Phalaropus lobatus*

The red-necked phalarope is a small wader that, unlike other waders, is frequently seen swimming. It sits high in the water and will spin like a top, dabbing at small insects and plankton that come to the surface. The female is larger and more brightly coloured than the male, and is the dominant partner during courtship. The male incubates the eggs and tends the young after hatching, while the females gather in flocks, more or less ignoring their offspring.

They are found in shallow pools and around the edges of larger ponds and lakes, and they build their nests in marshland, often some distance from water. Essentially an Arctic species, they are on the southern edge of their breeding range in Britain, occurring in the Hebrides, Shetland, possibly Orkney, and one or two places in mainland Scotland. They spend the winter at sea. Numbers fluctuate from 30 to 50 pairs, but otherwise seem fairly stable. The changing pattern of land-use, involving drainage of their preferred marshy pools, is a potential problem, but so far does not seem to have had any great effect. Though generally quite tame, they can be affected by disturbance during the breeding season, but are protected in Shetland reserves.

The species is very widespread, breeding around the world between about 60°N and 70°N. In North America it is called the 'northern' phalarope.

KINGSTON COLLEGE OF FURTHER EDUCATION LIBRARY

Pintail *Anas acuta*

The pintail is an elegant dabbling duck, the male being especially handsome, with his chocolate-coloured head, slender neck, and greatly elongated central tail-feathers, which extend to a point, or 'pin'.

It favours fairly shallow water in a variety of habitats including lakes, pools, marshes, fens, and moorland. Its nest – which is sometimes 50 to 200 yards from water – may be in short grass on open ground, or concealed in heather or long grass.

It is a fairly common visitor to Britain in winter, when it is found in estuaries and marshes in quite large concentrations, but it did not start to breed here until the last century. The first Scottish nest was recorded in 1869, and the first English one in 1910. Numbers have gradually increased, and now vary from 30 to 50 pairs. Distribution is very scattered, from Orkney through mainland Scotland to East Anglia and Kent. Nest sites are rarely occupied for more than a year or two in succession. It is specially protected under the Wildlife and Countryside Act during the close season, but may be shot at other times.

It is widely distributed around the northern latitudes of the world.

Little ringed plover   *Charadrius dubius*

The little ringed plover is a small shore bird, smaller than its close relative the ringed plover. Obvious differences between the two are the little ringed plover's yellow eye-ring, its plain brown upper wing, and its calls.

The little ringed plover's typical nesting habitat is shingle beds in rivers, but in Britain it mainly breeds at gravel pits and to some extent industrial tips and reservoirs. It was unknown as a breeding species until 1938, when a pair bred in Hertfordshire. Three more pairs bred in 1944, and since then numbers have risen sharply. In recent times they seem to have taken advantage of the country-wide increase in the number of gravel pits, which appears to be a determining factor in their breeding pattern.

They are now found from Northern England southwards through the Midlands and East Anglia, and in the London area, but are absent from Wales and the South-West. Numbers have passed the 400 mark and may still be increasing. The species also occurs widely across Europe and Asia.

Black redstart *Phoenicurus ochruros*

The black redstart is a chat with a distinctive rufous-coloured rump and tail; the name 'redstart' derives from an old English word *steort* meaning 'tail'. The male is greyish-black in colour.

Its favoured habitats are woodlands, gardens, mountain slopes and cliffs, but it has also adapted itself to the multitude of nesting sites available in urban areas. In Britain redstarts originally occurred as passage migrants during spring and autumn, with some birds over-wintering. They first bred here in the 1920s and continued to do so sporadically thereafter. A noticeable increase took place during and after the Second World War, when they colonised London's bomb sites. They nest in odd nooks and crannies, especially in old brick walls; also in sea cliffs.

Although the main colonisation took place in the 1940s when bomb sites were readily available, the true cause may have been overspill following a series of unusually good breeding seasons in Europe. The species has now spread to factories, power stations, railway sidings, and other similar sites, and is scattered across Central and Southern England, especially around London. Numbers are not great (probably fewer than 100 pairs) but seem stable.

It also occurs in Europe and eastwards to Central Asia and China.

Redwing   *Turdus iliacus*

The redwing is a small thrush which in some ways resembles the song thrush but has a conspicuous eye-stripe, and rusty red patches on its sides and under its wings. In winter it is commonly seen in mixed flocks with fieldfares.

It is a Northern European species found in birch forests and on the tundra among birch and willow scrub. In Britain it is restricted to Scotland, mainly the Highlands, where it nests in a great variety of habitats from woodlands to gardens. Though considerable numbers appear in Britain during the winter it was not known to breed here until discovered in Scotland in 1925. Thereafter it occurred intermittently up to the 1960s and '70s, when there was a notable increase, and it now seems to be an established breeding species. Numbers generally average up to 50 pairs a year, but have been known to reach several hundred pairs.

The origin of the Scottish redwing is uncertain. It may have been the result of invasive 'eruptions' of the Scandinavian population, though another theory is that migrants returning from Southern Europe to breed in Scandinavia were blown off course.

The species breeds across Northern Europe and Asia and in Iceland.

Ruff *Philomachus pugnax*

The ruff is a medium-sized wader that in winter may be confused with a redshank. However, the male in his breeding plumage (as in this photograph) is a remarkable sight and cannot be confused with any other bird. At this time of year he acquires an exotic neck-ruff of long feathers, and distinctive ear-tufts. Thus decked out, the males gather at 'leks' where they establish territories, and court the females (or 'reeves'). Their breeding grounds are on low-lying meadows and marshes, mostly in Eastern England and especially in the Ouse Washes.

The species was once quite widespread, but declined in the eighteenth and nineteenth centuries through drainage of its fenland habitat. It was also a popular dish and was extensively shot. When it became scarce, collectors moved in to take eggs and skins. For these various reasons, breeding came to an end for over seventy years, from the 1890s until 1963, when ruffs returned to the Ouse Washes. Since then they have increased and spread, though actual evidence of breeding is difficult to determine, as the nests and young are not easy to find. The principal sites are well protected.

Ruffs and reeves are also seen during their migrations to and from Africa. They breed across Northern Europe and Asia.

Wood sandpiper   *Tringa glareola*

The wood sandpiper is a long-legged wader quite similar to the green sandpiper, and may be regarded as a species intermediate between this and the common sandpiper.

It nests on the ground in damp places such as marshes and boggy moorland, and in conifer and birch forests. In Britain it is generally found near small lakes edged with reeds and sedges. It may sometimes take to living in the discarded nests of other birds.

It winters in Africa south of the Sahara, India, South-East Asia and Australia, returning north in the spring to breed. It occurs as a passage migrant in South-Eastern England, particularly in the autumn, but its normal breeding range is to the north and east of this country. There were isolated records of its breeding in the last century but none in this century, until 1959, when a pair bred in Sutherland. It has bred in most years since then in different parts of the Highlands, but is clearly a marginal breeding species.

There is no reason why it should not continue to breed here as long as suitable areas of wetland remain and nest locations are kept secret.

It also occurs from Scandinavia eastwards to the Pacific.

Common scoter   *Melanitta nigra*

The common scoter is a diving sea duck which tends to form dense flocks – either congregating on suitable stretches of water, or flying low over the surface in long, uneven lines. The male is all-black, while the female is brown and buff. The name 'scoter' may come from an Old English word *sceotar* meaning 'to move rapidly', in which case it may have the same derivation as 'scoot'. In France the scoter was once considered suitable food for Lent, as it fed on fish; in fact it feeds on mussels and other molluscs. When diving to the sea-bed it opens its wings to stabilise itself.

It breeds near small moorland lochs, and also by Loch Lomond. It appears to have colonised Scotland in the middle of the nineteenth century, and has spread slowly to various parts of the Highlands and Islands, with perhaps 20 to 30 pairs nesting every year.

This gregarious species is a northern bird that comes to British waters in large numbers in winter. Though normally found offshore, it sometimes enters estuaries and occasionally visits inland reservoirs. It also occurs from Scandinavia across Eurasia, and in North America.

Serin *Serinus serinus*

The serin is a small finch from the woodland fringes of the Mediterranean. It is closely related to the wild canary, *Serinus canaria*, of the Azores and Canary Islands, from which the cage bird is descended.

Its original natural habitat is deciduous woodland, but it is now commonly found in parks, gardens, orchards and other habitats associated with man. It has been spreading northwards from the Mediterranean for at least two centuries.

Its eventual arrival in Britain was to be expected, and it was seen quite frequently after 1960: the first breeding record having been in Dorset in 1967. Two or three pairs now breed in South-ern England, though in some years there may be none. It remains to be seen whether the serin will continue its northwards advance and consolidate its foothold here.

It is a comparatively tame bird, but one that could pass unnoticed in places such as municipal parks and out-of-the-way villages. The non-expert might confuse it with the siskin, which is also a yellowish-green finch with dark streaking.

Red-backed shrike *Lanius collurio*

The red-backed shrike is a predatory bird with a hooked bill which feeds on large invertebrates such as moths, bees, grasshoppers, and dragonflies; also a variety of small mammals, birds, amphibians, and reptiles. It has the habit of storing up a supply of food by impaling the corpses of its prey on thorns or barbed wire. There is an old belief that it kills nine times before it begins to eat, and in Germany it is still known as the *neuntöter* or 'nine-killer'.

It is found in areas where there are scattered, mature bushes. Its range in Britain was once widespread – from Lancashire and Cumberland southwards – but has gradually contracted to an area of East Anglia and parts of Southern England. A similar decline has been taking place in Western Europe, and in both cases it could be due to wetter summers and destruction of habitat. In Britain the species appears to be at a watershed, as there are now only 20 to 25 breeding pairs compared with over 300 in 1952. However, an intriguing possibility is that Scandinavian birds may be on the point of colonising Scotland, where one or two pairs have been seen in recent years.

As well as the red-backed shrikes that breed here, flocks of them can be seen in the autumn en route to their winter quarters in East and South Africa. They also breed across Europe and Asia to Japan.

Temminck's stint *Calidris temminckii*

Temminck's stint is a small wader, about the size of a house sparrow: 'stint' is a diminutive name which from the fifteenth century has been applied to some of the smaller waders. In appearance Temminck's resembles a common sandpiper, whereas its relative the little stint is more like a dunlin. When disturbed it rises sharply into the air; and it is less inclined than other waders to congregate in mixed flocks.

It inhabits marshes and bogs, and in Finland, according to O. Hilden, a Finnish ornithologist, a remarkable double-clutch strategy has been observed: 'Every female pairs in rapid succession with two males on different territories and lays one clutch in each. Every male also pairs successively on the same territory with two females and fertilises one clutch of each.' This has not yet been observed in Britain.

Temminck's stint first nested successfully in Scotland in 1971, and now some seven or eight pairs breed in three or four sites. The fact that the adults are relatively long-lived, combined with their high reproductive potential, suggests that the species could become firmly established.

The main breeding range is in the tundra from Norway eastwards to the Bering Strait.

Black tern   *Chlidonias niger*

The black tern is distinguished from other terns by its entirely black head and underparts. When breeding, it is also found in a different habitat from other terns in Britain, for it is a marsh bird, nesting inland in marshes, fens and other waterways rather than by the sea shore. It feeds on various aquatic insects and their larvae, and occasionally small fish, which it catches when skimming the surface of the water, rather than by diving.

It was once abundant in Eastern and South-Eastern England but declined when its habitat was drained to provide more agricultural land. It seems not to have bred in Britain for almost 100 years, from 1858 until 1966, when two pairs laid eggs in the Ouse Washes. Since then it has bred intermittently, but only when conditions, such as the water level, are suitable.

It is a regular visitor to Eastern and Southern England during its migration to and from tropical Africa, when it may be seen in the coastal habitat more commonly favoured by its species.

It occurs in temperate zones of Europe and Asia, and in North America.

Little tern *Sterna albifrons*

This is the smallest tern found in Britain. It breeds in coastal areas, congregating in small colonies and nesting in sand or shingle, at or close to the shoreline. It has a somewhat jerky flight with rapid wing beats, and may often be seen hovering before diving for food. It tends to feed inshore, or in creeks and shallow coastal lagoons.

Its nest-scrapes are vulnerable to a variety of natural factors, including obliteration by sand in strong winds, destruction by high tides and storms, and depredation by foxes. It is also subject to egg-collecting and disturbance by holiday-makers.

The population declined during the nineteenth century, but more recently, despite fluctuations, has tended to increase, and is now fairly stable at around 2,100 pairs. Most of the breeding population occurs in reserves of some kind. Though this species has benefited considerably from conservation measures, it will probably always need protection if it is to maintain its numbers.

It breeds in many parts of the world. The British breeders winter on the coast of West Africa.

Roseate tern *Sterna dougallii*

The roseate tern is our most endangered breeding seabird. It is similar to the common and Arctic terns, but has especially long and graceful tail-streamers. The rosy-pink flush on its breast (hence 'roseate') is visible only for a short time in the spring, and then at close quarters.

It nests on rocky or sandy offshore islands and sometimes in estuaries, usually in mixed colonies with other terns. Its recognition as a distinct species, in 1812, signalled the start of heavy persecution by egg- and skin-collectors, and therefore a decline in its numbers. It is vulnerable to flooding of its nests during storms and high tides, and to disturbance by visitors. Also, many roseate terns are trapped for food in their winter quarters on the coast of West Africa.

After a decline lasting more than a hundred years, there was a significant increase in numbers in this century: in the 1960s there may have been 3,500 breeding pairs in Britain and Ireland. However, numbers today are reduced to about 300 pairs in Britain (all in reserves) and 600 in Ireland. Similar declines have been recorded in Europe and North America. The species has a scattered distribution in other parts of the world.

Bearded tit   *Panurus biarmicus*

The bearded tit is not really a tit at all but is related to the family of babblers. It is also called the 'bearded reedling' after its habitat, which consists exclusively of reed-beds, where it feeds on insects and seeds. In the days when much of Eastern England consisted of marshes and fens it was widespread, but extensive drainage destroyed much of its habitat.

In the nineteenth century, egg- and skin-collectors, as well as trappers capturing bearded tits for sale as cage birds, seriously reduced its numbers. It can also be badly affected by hard winters: not so much by cold weather as by heavy snowfalls and ice, which make the reed seeds inaccessible. In 1946 to 1947 the species was reduced to a handful of birds in East Anglia, but has since recovered. Numbers still fluctuate but probably average several hundred pairs, which are found in East Anglia, Southern England, and in the RSPB reserve at Leighton Moss in Lancashire.

It has a high reproductive potential – sometimes producing two or even three broods in a season – and this combined with the present reasonably high numbers suggests that so long as reed-bed habitat remains it will be able to survive even the severest winters.

It also occurs quite widely across Europe and Asia.

Crested tit *Parus cristatus*

The crested tit is easily identified by its prominent chequered crest, for it is the only very small bird that has this distinctive feature. It inhabits mature forests of Scots pine, nesting in holes that it makes in decaying wood, and feeding on insects, pine seeds, and berries.

It was probably fairly widespread when there were extensive pine forests, but declined from the Middle Ages onwards as the forests were felled. It is now found only in the Central Highlands, especially in the Spey valley. There may be 1,000 pairs, and there seems to be some evidence of recent colonisation of new sites.

It might be thought that the proliferation of large conifer plantations in Britain in recent times would have encouraged more widespread breeding, but the crested tit will not settle in to plantations until they are about 20 years old, and then only if it can find dead trees. It is also a very sedentary bird, so colonisation, either from Scotland southwards, or from Europe (where it is widespread) apparently does not take place.

Cetti's warbler   *Cettia cetti*

Cetti's warbler is a small bird, not unlike a nightingale, but drabber in colour and lacking the latter's prominent tail. As it is unobtrusive, it is not easy to see, but can be located by its extremely loud song, uttered in strident, staccato bursts.

It breeds among thick, tangled vegetation in wet places such as marshes, reed-beds and willow and alder carr. It is essentially a bird of the Mediterranean region but has been spreading northwards since the turn of the century, its advance checked but not halted by severe winters. By the 1960s it had reached Belgium and Holland. In 1972 it was recorded for the first time as breeding in Britain. Having established a foothold in Kent, it has spread north to East Anglia and west to several other southern English counties. It is a resident rather than a migrant species, so it has colonised new areas gradually. Its numbers continue to increase, and since there appears to be plenty of suitable habitat it seems likely that this very successful new colonist may expand its range considerably and eventually become common.

It occurs across Europe and North Africa, and eastwards as far as Afghanistan.

Dartford warbler   *Sylvia undata*

The Dartford warbler is an elusive bird which rarely leaves the shelter of its habitat, except in spring, when the males can be seen as well as heard. Its name is derived from Dartford in Kent, where it was first recorded as a British breeding species in 1773. It has long since disappeared from that region.

It is restricted to areas of lowland heath, especially where gorse and mature heather are plentiful. As a resident species which remains in its breeding areas throughout the year, it is vulnerable to severe winters, when the insects and spiders on which it feeds are greatly reduced.

The major threat to its numbers is the disappearance and fragmentation of its habitat, which is liable to be encroached upon by trees, as well as being subject to destruction for commercial and agricultural development. In 1961 there were some 460 pairs recorded, but by 1963 these had been reduced to about a dozen. Encouragingly, however, it seems able to recover its numbers, and there are now some 550 pairs.

The species breeds mainly in Hampshire and Dorset, also in Mediterranean areas and other parts of Western Europe.

Marsh warbler *Acrocephalus palustris*

The marsh warbler is very similar in appearance to the much commoner reed warbler, but can be identified by its song which is much more melodious than that of its relative. A particularly distinctive feature is its near-perfect mimicry of the song of other birds – a repertoire covering some 50 different species, including waders, terns and game-birds. Anyone hearing such a variety of sounds coming from one bush might deduce that it was the work of this extraordinary bird.

Despite its name, it nests in relatively dry areas, though usually near water and especially among nettles, meadowsweet or hoary willow-herb. Osier-beds were once its most favoured habitat, but they are now only to be found in a few nature reserves, where they are carefully tended. As the osier-beds have disappeared, so the population of the marsh warbler has declined. It now occurs in small numbers (probably fewer than 100 pairs) in a few pockets along the Severn Valley in Worcestershire.

The species also breeds across Europe and into Western Russia.

Savi's warbler *Locustella luscinioides*

Savi's warbler is similar to the grass-hopper and reed warblers, but is slightly larger. It is also somewhat easier to locate, since it often sings from the top of reeds or bushes or other prominent song-posts.

It nests in wet places, generally in reed-beds with an undergrowth of sedges. At one time, apparently, it bred in the vast marshes and fens of Norfolk, Suffolk, Cambridgeshire and Hunting-donshire, but became extinct as a breed-ing species in the mid-nineteenth cen-tury, probably through drainage of its habitat. However, during this century it began to expand its range in Europe, and by 1960 had re-colonised Britain, spreading out from its original site in Kent to a number of southern and eastern English counties. It appears not to have progressed beyond this initial stage of colonisation, and its numbers remain small – some 20 pairs breeding each year. The population seems to be stable.

It is a migratory species, leaving in July for its winter quarters in Africa. It also breeds in scattered sites across Europe and eastward to Siberia.

Whimbrel *Numenius phaeopus*

The whimbrel is a large wader which is similar to the curlew, but smaller and with a shorter bill. Its name may be derived from its distinctive call, which consists of seven high-pitched tremulous whistles, said to be reminiscent of the whimpering of hounds.

It breeds at higher altitudes and latitudes than the curlew, and in areas where the two species overlap the whimbrel nests on hillsides and the curlew in the valleys. It is found in moorland, usually among dry grass and heather, but sometimes on boggy ground. In Britain it is on the southern edge of its range.

Numbers declined in the latter part of the nineteenth century and the beginning of the twentieth, perhaps because of climatic changes. This trend has now been reversed, and nearly 200 pairs have been recorded, mostly in Shetland, but also on some other Scottish islands and occasionally on the mainland. The increase has been concurrent with a series of cooler springs. The population seems stable but could be affected by any major changes in land-use in Shetland.

In other parts of the world the whimbrel breeds at high latitudes, from Iceland across Scandinavia, Northern Russia and North America.

Woodlark   *Lullula arborea*

The woodlark is similar in appearance to the much commoner skylark, but has a shorter tail. Its fluent, melodic song is warmer in tone than that of the skylark, though rather less varied.

It needs short grass in which to feed on insects and seeds; longer grass for nesting; and trees, bushes or even fencing for use as song-posts. These requirements are found in heathland, commons, or wooded parkland.

In the past the species may have bred in every county of England and Wales, but it has declined through loss of habitat, especially heathland and grass, which, until recently, was cropped short by rabbits. However, it has the ability to exploit woodland in the early stages of regeneration after felling.

It is now restricted to East Anglia and parts of Southern England, where there are between 200 and 450 pairs. It has also been declining in Northern Europe, and there are theories that as well as habitat loss, some other factor, such as long-term climatic changes, might be the cause.

It is predominantly a European species, extending to Turkey and North Africa.

Wryneck   *Jynx torquilla*

The wryneck belongs to the same family as the woodpecker, though it does not climb tree trunks. It spends much of the time on the ground, flicking out its long tongue to catch ants, its principal food. It is something of a contortionist, having the ability to twist its head sideways and to bend it backwards through 180 degrees.

It prefers open woodland, parkland, orchards, and other areas with suitable tree holes for nesting, and relatively short grass where it can find ants. Though once quite common in England, it has been declining and contracting its range southwards for 150 years, to the point where it has now vanished altogether. Many reasons have been suggested for this but the main one is probably the climatic change which has given rise to cool, cloudy summers, thus reducing the supply of ants. The species has also been declining in Western Europe, perhaps for the same reason. Conversely, the climatic change seems to have caused Scandinavian birds to colonise Northern Scotland, where some half dozen pairs now breed regularly.

The wryneck winters in Africa, where continental birds are frequently found on the east coast during migration. It also occurs from Europe east to Japan.

Great crested newt *Triturus cristatus*

The great crested or 'warty' newt is the largest British newt, with adults generally reaching five and a half inches in length, including the tail. Males develop a prominent crest during the breeding season. The alternative name of 'warty' derives from the rough, rather coarse skin on the newt's upper parts.

It is relatively aquatic and may be found in the water at any time of the year, although it usually hibernates on land. It prefers still water, with plenty of vegetation for breeding, while on land it seems to need quite dense shrubs at the water's edge. It is fairly widely distributed in England, but is absent in most of the south-west. It is also absent from most of Scotland and Wales. The species occurs in Northern and Central Europe and eastwards to Iran.

This species appears to be declining rapidly in Britain (and also across a large part of Northern Europe). A recent survey of lowland England has shown that breeding sites are being lost at the rate of five per cent per year.

The great crested newt cannot long survive the introduction of predatory fish to a pond, nor can it tolerate excessive numbers of wildfowl (as in ornamental ponds) which quickly disrupt the ecological balance. The species is not good at colonising new ponds without human aid.

Palmate newt *Triturus helveticus*

The palmate newt is a fairly small, smooth-skinned species. During the breeding season the male develops webbed, hand-like feet. The females are larger than the males. This newt is somewhat similar to the smooth newt, and the females especially look alike. The two species are sometimes found together, and hybrids have been bred in captivity, suggesting that in the past they might have diverged from a single ancestral species.

The palmate newt spends parts of each year on land, where it usually (but not always) hibernates; at this time it is rather secretive. It breeds in a variety of still-water habitats, including ponds, pools, and puddles, and even brackish water near the sea. It tends to thrive in rather clear and acid ponds in moorland and upland areas, and is less often found in hard-water areas. It is widely distributed in Britain, especially in Southern and Northern England, Wales, and parts of Scotland. It is also found in Europe from the Atlantic to Switzerland.

In common with other amphibians, the palmate newt has declined as ponds have disappeared or become degraded, but its ability to thrive in rather acid water gives it an advantage over other species. It is not threatened nationally but is declining locally. It is protected only in respect of trade.

Smooth newt   *Triturus vulgaris*

The smooth newt is the most widespread amphibian in Britain. Adults may be more than four inches long, including the tail, and the males are generally slightly larger than the females. In the breeding season the male is a handsome sight, with dark spots on the upper surface, a continuous crest along the body and tail, fringes on the toes of the hind feet, and a bright orange, spotted belly.

It is more terrestrial than most other newts and favours damp habitats, such as gardens, woods, field edges and heaps of stones. It breeds in still and quite shallow water, especially weedy ponds and ditches, and tends to be a lowland species. It is very widely distributed in England, though it is less common in the South-West and is scarce in South and West Wales. In Scotland it occurs most frequently in the Central Lowlands. It is also found over most of Europe and into Western Asia.

It seems well able to tolerate habitat disturbance, and can readily colonise new ponds. It thrives in suburbia and does not take long to find a newly created garden pond. It copes much less successfully in arable farming country. It is protected only in respect of trade.

Common frog *Rana temporaria*

The common frog is a member of the large Ranidae family of true frogs. Adults are about three inches long. The species is very variable in colour and markings, though the background colour is predominantly brownish. Reddish-coloured frogs can sometimes be seen in Scotland, and the females seem more often to be red than the males. They may gather in larger numbers to breed, when the males sing in chorus, and develop 'nuptial pads' on their thumbs. They are found in damp vegetation in a variety of habitats, even up to the snow-line, and often some distance from the breeding site. They are widespread throughout Britain except on some outlying islands; also throughout Northern and Central Europe and mainland Asia.

The species was once thought to be declining, but now appears to be making a comeback, perhaps helped by the wetter weather of the past several years.

It thrives in suburbia, but does not do so well in arable farmland. The large numbers used by schools and colleges for biology instruction was a threat in the past, but dissection is now being phased out, especially in schools. The species is protected only in respect of trade.

Common toad *Bufo bufo*

The common toad is a member of the Bufonidae family, or 'typical' toads. It may grow to nearly four inches in length, the female being larger then the male. Its colour is generally brownish but there are many variations, ranging from sandy through red to greyish. The common toad has marked warty bumps on its skin, and compared with the common frog its hind legs are better adapted to walking than leaping.

This species is found in a variety of often quite dry habitats outside the breeding season. It is mainly nocturnal and spends the day hiding in a hole in the ground or under logs, bark, etc. It is seldom eaten by predators since its skin is toxic. It is found across most of Britain but not in Ireland. It also occurs in Europe, Asia, and North Africa.

It is most vulnerable at the start of the breeding season, when large numbers converge on the breeding sites. They may travel for two miles, and are frequently squashed on roads: males sometimes sit waiting for unmated females to pass by, which adds to their chances of getting killed.

The species seems strongly tied to its ancestral breeding sites, and does not readily colonise new ponds. It is vulnerable nationally, though it may be locally endangered. It is protected only in respect of trade.

Natterjack toad *Bufo calamita*

The natterjack, a typical toad of the Bufonidae family, is Britain's rarest and most endangered amphibian. It is about two and a half inches long and its hind legs are much shorter than those of the common toad or the frog. It cannot hop, but tends to run rather fast in short bursts, giving rise to another common name, the 'running toad'.

It lives in heathlands and among dune systems, where during the daytime hours and also for hibernation it burrows easily into the sandy soil. It spawns in shallow pools, and during the breeding season (April–June) a loud croaking chorus of males can be heard.

It now survives in two heathland sites (one in Hampshire, one in East Anglia), and on coastal dunes in East Anglia and the North-West: its main stronghold being a stretch of dunes in Lancashire.

It has declined rapidly during this century because of massive destruction and alteration of its habitat for development of various kinds, which in coastal areas includes recreational amenities. Most of its remaining sites are protected, and it is found in several National Nature Reserves.

It also occurs in Western and Central Europe and in South-West Ireland.

Sand lizard *Lacerta agilis*

The sand lizard belongs to the group which because of their colour are known as green lizards. Though the male has greenish flanks – which are especially bright in the breeding season – the female is rarely green. In fact, the colouring is very variable, and in this country those from Southern England are darker than those from the North.

It is a stocky, short-legged reptile some seven to eight inches long, including its tail, which is longer than its body. It spends much of its time in underground burrows, where it also hibernates. It needs fairly dense vegetation as well as bare sand for egg-laying, which takes place in June and July.

The species lives in colonies in a wide variety of habitats, but in Britain is found only on coastal sand dunes from Liverpool to Southport, and on mature lowland heaths in Dorset, Hampshire and Surrey. It once occurred more widely in the South and North-West, and in Wales.

It is most vulnerable in the northern dunes, where there may be fewer than 200 surviving. But its heathland habitat is also threatened – by ploughing, afforestation, development of various kinds, and fires. The number of heathland colonies declined from 166 in 1970 to 44 in 1980.

The species is seriously endangered, and without careful protection could be extinct during the next decade. It occurs in much of Europe eastwards into Asia.

Viviparous lizard *Lacerta vivipara*

The viviparous or common lizard is a small member of the Lacertidae family, measuring up to seven inches long. The tail is sometimes twice as long as the body. Its basic colour is brownish, though the belly may be white, yellow, or orange, especially in breeding males. It usually gives birth to fully formed young, hence 'viviparous', but sometimes lays eggs. The number of young varies from three to twelve.

It is a more northerly species than the sand lizard, and although it likes to bask in the sun, it does so for a shorter time than the latter. During very hot weather it keeps out of the sun altogether.

It is preyed upon by a variety of vertebrate animals. Shrews, though they may take young lizards, try to avoid encounters with the adults, which when alarmed have been known to scream like a shrew.

The viviparous lizard is found in a great variety of habitats, including bogs, woodland, hedgerows, field edges, heaths, grassland, and sand dunes.

It is widespread in Britain and Ireland, and on a number of islands. It is not endangered, though it has declined in some areas. It is also taken in large numbers by domestic cats. It is listed in the Wildlife and Countryside Act in respect of trade only.

It is found across most of North and Central Europe and Asia to the Sea of Japan.

Slow-worm   *Anguis fragilis*

The slow-worm is a legless lizard of the Anguidae family, most of whose members have either very short legs or none at all. Its name derives from the slowness of its movements and its resemblance to a snake ('worm' was an Old English word for snake).

Slow-worms are secretive and inconspicuous and not a great deal is known about their life in the wild. They are ovoviviparous, that is the egg membrane ruptures at birth or shortly afterwards. From 6 to 12 young are born around the end of August. They are long-lived (up to 50 years in captivity).

The slow-worm lives in rough grass-land, woodland glades, and often in damp places such as leaf litter. It is found as far north as the Outer Hebrides, and is widely distributed in Southern England.

Though it does not seem to be endangered nationally, its preferred habitat of rough ground is gradually disappearing, and it is on the decline in some areas. It does not flourish in suburbia, where it is easy prey for cats. It is listed in the Wildlife and Countryside Act in respect of trade only.

It is found throughout Europe and as far east as Iran, as well as in North Africa.

178

Adder *Vipera berus*

The adder, or northern viper, is one of the true vipers, of which there are eight species in Europe. It generally grows to about two feet in length and can be identified by the dark zig-zag line along its back. It also has a V-shaped mark on its head. All-black adders are sometimes found. It is active by day and swims well.

The adder is the only venomous snake in Britain. The venom is expelled through long, hollow fangs which when not in use are folded back against the roof of the mouth. It feeds mainly on small mammals and other reptiles, though it also takes young birds and some invertebrates. It is not aggressive unless disturbed. Its venom fangs are primarily for hunting prey, but can be used defensively. Only ten people have died from adder bites in Britain during the last hundred years, and even dogs that are bitten seldom die: far more people die from bee or wasp stings.

The species is widely distributed in a broad range of habitats throughout Britain. It is not endangered, though it is rarer than it used to be in some areas, especially lowland England. It is persecuted because of its reputation as a dangerous snake, and is affected by the disappearance of its preferred rough habitat. It is listed in the Wildlife and Countryside Act in respect of trade only.

It occurs across Europe and Asia to China, and even into the Arctic.

Grass snake   *Natrix natrix*

The grass snake belongs to the Colubridae family and is the largest British snake, growing to about four feet in length. It has also been called the 'collared' or 'ringed' snake. It is active by day but is rather shy, and tends to move rapidly into cover when a human approaches. It is the most aquatic of British snakes and is often seen swimming, diving, or basking at the water's edge. Even in predominantly dry habitats it prefers boggy places.

From 10 to 40 eggs are laid, often in communal sites, in warm, moist places such as a pile of manure, a compost heap, or a hayrick. The eggs hatch towards the end of August, the young using their 'egg tooth' to cut through the egg membrane. It feeds mainly on frogs and fish, which it catches when swimming. But it also takes lizards, toads, and even small mammals and birds. It is not venomous.

It is quite widely distributed in England and Wales but not in Scotland, and seems to be declining everywhere, mainly due to the lack of suitable egg-laying sites. It is also killed by people who mistake it for an adder. It is listed in the Act only in respect of trade.

It is found throughout Europe, North Africa and Western Asia.

Smooth snake   *Coronella austriaca*

The smooth snake, which belongs to the large Colubridae family, is the rarest and most endangered of British snakes. It grows to a length of about two feet, and is slender in shape and greyish-brown in colour, with rows of small black flecks on its back. Though active by day, it is slow-moving and rather secretive. It is said to be quite intelligent for a snake, and will sometimes take refuge in water when threatened.

A constrictor, enveloping prey in its coils, it feeds on lizards – especially the sand lizard – but will also eat other reptiles, including snakes, and sometimes small mammals and insects.

It occurs in the same dry, sandy heathland as the sand lizard, favouring open heath, preferably without trees. It is now found only in small areas of Dorset, Hampshire and Surrey, and is threatened by the disappearance and fragmentation of its heathland habitat, through development, afforestation and burning. It is also killed by man, and is likely to have been affected by the decline in numbers of the sand lizard.

It occurs in most of Europe, but is declining in the Northern and Western parts of its range.

Burbot *Lota lota*

The burbot, sometimes called the 'eel-pout', is the only freshwater member of the cod family. Measuring about fifteen inches and weighing a pound at around six years old, it can reach three feet in length and weighs up to sixty pounds.

It is active only around dawn and dusk; during the day it hides under rocks, roots, or in holes in the bank. It feeds on mussels, snails, crustaceans, and other fish such as perch, roach, and gudgeon. It lives at the bottom of cool, clear lakes and rivers, and spawns over gravel, sand, or hard clay, while the young fish like to live among dense reed-beds.

It once occurred in eastern rivers, from Durham to Suffolk, and perhaps in the Thames, but is now extremely rare, if not extinct, in Britain. The last record was from Suffolk in the late 1970s. Its recent decline has been due to destruction of its habitat by the scouring and canalisation of rivers. Suitable habitat may no longer exist.

Though its flesh is as good to eat as that of the cod, it is now seldom caught in Western Europe. It is quite common in Asia and North America, and is still commercially important in the USSR.

Fen raft spider   *Dolomedes plantarius*

The fen raft spider is said to be the largest British spider, with a body length of around an inch. It was first discovered here in 1956. It feeds on anything that it can catch, on land or in and under the water. It is found in one locality in Suffolk, in vegetation surrounding small pools and water-filled peat diggings.

At one time the existence of this spectacular creature was threatened by plans to increase water abstraction by sinking boreholes in the area where it is found. This would have lowered the water level and would probably have caused the extinction of the spider. However, the problem was pointed out to the Anglian Water Authority and the threat was averted. More recently, ponds have been specially dug for it, and the spider seems to have taken to them. It occurs within one Nature Conservation Trust Reserve.

Ladybird spider   *Eresus niger*

The ladybird spider is the only species of the Eresidae family in Britain and belongs to the group of lace-web spiders. The female is a sombre velvety black and about half an inch long. The male is rather smaller but more richly coloured, with three pairs of round black spots edged with white hairs on its orange-red abdomen. It was the male's appearance that inspired the name – which in fact was specifically devised for the Wildlife and Countryside Act, as each scheduled species was required to have a common name.

This spider lives in or at the edges of heather in Southern England. It is also found in Europe. The species has always been very rare in Britain, and between 1816 and 1906 only six males and one female were found. Since then, none was seen until quite recently when some were discovered during the course of a heathland research project.

As the male ladybird spider is particularly eyecatching, it could be sought after by collectors.

Large blue butterfly *Maculinea arion*

The large blue belongs to the Lycaenidae family, which also includes the coppers and hairstreaks. It is about an inch and a half across with wings spread.

It has a most unusual life cycle. The eggs are laid on wild thyme in July and the caterpillars feed on the flowers. But soon they start to secrete a honeydew-like substance that attracts red ants. The ants carry the caterpillars into their nests, where they feed on ant larvae, until they emerge as butterflies the following June or July.

The large blue frequents rough grassy places, often near the sea. There were once a number of colonies in the Cotswolds and in Somerset, Devon, and Cornwall. But by 1970 all except one colony in Devon had disappeared because of intensified farming and the extermination by myxomatosis of rabbits, which had kept the turf closely grazed. Several dry summers followed and in spite of management of the site, by 1979 the species was declared extinct (though it still exists in parts of Europe).

It is said to survive in the Cotswolds, but no reputable entomologist has been able to confirm this claim. The Nature Conservancy Council in association with the World Wildlife Fund is considering the introduction of large blues from Europe. But first they have to see if the European insects will accept British thyme, and whether our ants will take the European caterpillars to their nests.

Swallowtail butterfly   *Papilio machaon*

The swallowtail is the only British member of the large and showy Papilionidae family. It is also our biggest resident butterfly, measuring over two and a half inches with wings outstretched.

The British swallowtail is a distinct race, with a darker appearance than its European counterparts. It flies in May and June, and a small second brood may also emerge in August.

The species in general is found in various habitats up to about 6,000 feet, and its food plants include wild carrot, fennel, and wild angelica. It is widely distributed from North Africa to North Cape, and across Europe and Asia to Japan. The paler European swallowtails sometimes reach Southern England, and may survive for a season or two. The British swallowtail is confined to low-lying fenland.

The species is at present holding its own, with a number of healthy populations in Eastern England. Although as yet there is no cause for concern, it is a localised species and in the Norfolk Broads it faces a potential threat from encroaching scrub. It is also vulnerable to changes in water level that can cause subtle alterations in its habitat.

It occurs in several National Nature Reserves and other protected sites.

Chequered skipper butterfly   *Carterocephalus palaemon*

The chequered skipper is one of eight British members of the Hesperidae, a primitive, fast-flying, and very moth-like family of butterflies.

The caterpillar hatches in June and feeds on various grasses, especially brome grass. It lives in a kind of tent made from blades of grass drawn together with silk, from where it can catapult its droppings some distance to conceal their presence. It passes the winter in the caterpillar stage, which is rare among butterflies, and the adults emerge the following May or June. It favours woodland glades and edges, where it is attracted by bugle flowers.

The species was once quite numerous, with about fifty colonies in the East Midlands, but a rapid decline began in the 1960s, and by 1975 it was extinct in England. This may have resulted from its habitat becoming too heavily shaded. Fortunately it was discovered in Inverness-shire in 1942, where it still survives in fair numbers.

It occurs in several National Nature Reserves.

Heath fritillary   *Mellicta athalia*

The heath fritillary is a small butterfly of the Nymphalidae family. The caterpillars hatch in July and feed mainly on common cow-wheat. They live gregariously beneath the leaves in a loose web, where they also hibernate. They feed again in the spring, before pupation. The adults are on the wing during June and July.

The species lives in woodland glades and thrives on coppice. Once fairly widespread in Southern England it has been affected by the conversion from coppice to conifers, and is now confined to colonies in Devon, Cornwall, and Kent. If there is a further decline in its habitat, the heath fritillary could soon become extinct. It occurs in one National Nature Reserve and is now our most endangered butterfly.

It is fairly common and widespread in Northern Europe.

Barberry carpet moth *Pareulype berberata*

The barberry carpet moth is a small member of the Larentiinae sub-family, which is part of the large group called Geometers. It flies in May and early June, and then again in August. Its stoutish caterpillars are brown, with indistinct, darker stripes along the back; they feed in June and July, on barberry, a flowering shrub. A second brood appears in late August and September.

Natural breeding occurs in only one hedgerow in East Anglia, but the moth has been introduced into a few other sites in Southern England. Its status is probably linked to that of its food plant and its habitat: barberry is not particularly common, and nowadays hedges are highly vulnerable to disturbance and destruction.

Though at present the barberry carpet moth seems to be holding its own, by virtue of its small numbers it is certainly endangered.

Black-veined moth *Siona lineata*

The black-veined moth is a small member of the Geometrinae sub-family of the Geometers, and appears from late May until the end of June. It flies in the sunshine and rests among long grass. Its long caterpillar is greyish in colour with several irregular darker lines on the back and sides.

Very little is known about this species, and even its food plant has not been identified. In captivity its caterpillars have been recorded as feeding on knotgrass, dock, bird's-foot trefoil, and other plants. In the wild, the female moths have been seen to deposit eggs on certain wood grasses.

It is very rare in Britain, and is known to exist in only about half a dozen sites in South-Eastern England (particularly Kent), most of them containing small populations.

It is also found in Europe and Asia. Research is in progress to discover more about its ecology.

Essex emerald moth   *Thetidia smaragdaria*

The Essex emerald is a small moth belonging to the Hemitheinae sub-family of the Geometers. It has the green colour typical of the emeralds, with white lines across its fore-wings, though sometimes these are absent. Its caterpillar covers itself with fragments of its food plant, sea wormwood, and is thus quite effectively camouflaged. The moth flies in June and early July, and the caterpillars appear in September.

The Essex emerald has a very restricted range in Britain, among the salt marshes of Essex. For a period it was thought to be extinct, but now one colony is definitely known, and there are reports of two other possible sites. It is also found in Europe and eastward to Siberia.

It is highly vulnerable to changes in its habitat, especially destruction of its food plant. Threats include reclamation of salt marshes on the Thames estuary,

improvement of sea-walls, and grazing by horses – though it is surprising that horses should want to eat such a strong-tasting plant as sea wormwood.

Museum specimen

New Forest burnet moth   *Zygaena viciae*

The New Forest burnet belongs to the Zygaenidae family, known in Britain as burnets and foresters. The species was first discovered here in 1869 when a number of very localised colonies were found in the New Forest.

Sometimes this species does not complete its growth cycle until it has spent two winters as a chrysalis. At the caterpillar stage, all members of the burnet family are a similar pale green in colour, and it is difficult to distinguish one particular species from the other. The New Forest species feeds on trefoils, especially the common bird's-foot, and clovers. The moth emerges in June and early July.

In the early part of this century entomological dealers staked out plots in the New Forest and, because the moths live in colonies and are naturally slow to fly away, the population was heavily reduced. This resulted ultimately in extinction. However, a few years ago one very small colony was discovered in Scotland, and its location is a closely-guarded secret.

The New Forest burnet can also be found in some parts of Europe.

Reddish buff moth

Acosmetia caliginosa

The reddish buff moth is a rather drab member of the Noctuidae, a large family of small or medium-sized moths. (There are some 400 Noctuids in Britain.) They are generally nocturnal, and the caterpillars also feed during the night. Their favoured food is thought to be sawwort, a relative of the cornflower.

Few people can claim to have seen this moth, which emerges in July, and nothing much is known about it. Apparently it does not visit flowers of any kind, and is not attracted by the sugary mixture that is often daubed on tree trunks to entice moths.

It has always been rare, and is apparently restricted to one locality in Southern England. In common with many other wildlife species it is threatened by the decline of coppicing and by the conversion of broadleafed woodland into conifer forest.

Museum specimen

Rainbow leaf beetle

Chrysolina cerealis

The rainbow leaf beetle is a member of the large Chrysomelidae family, of which there are some 250 species in Britain. The infamous and, fortunately, seldom seen Colorado beetle belongs to this family. As can be inferred from their name, these beetles commonly feed on leaves. The rainbow leaf species has a preference for wild thyme.

It is one of the few insects whose range is restricted to North Wales, where it is found in one well-established locality in Snowdonia and two other subsidiary sites. It has probably always been rare, but it still seems to be holding its own. Though few people hunt beetles today, it is attractive enought to tempt the occasional collector. Fortunately it is not subject to any other threats.

189

Norfolk aeshna dragonfly *Aeshna isosceles*

The Norfolk aeshna dragonfly is one of seven members of the Aeshnidae family occurring in Britain. All the aeshnas have long bodies, and they fly up and down their regular stretches of water for hours at a time. The Norfolk species frequents lowland ditches and ponds with still water and plenty of aquatic vegetation. It is now found at only three sites in the Norfolk Broads, an area that used to be the most extensive dragonfly habitat in Britain. Large parts of the Broads have been severely degraded, and most of the waterways, where once the air was alive with a myriad dragonflies, have now become sterile places. The Norfolk aeshna is very vulnerable to intensive management of agricultural land, including the scooping out of ditches and the lowering of water levels – changes associated with conversion of farmland from grazing to cereal-growing. In the last twenty-five years Britain has lost a tenth of its dragonflies – a greater loss than that of any other animal group.

Wart-biter grasshopper *Decticus verrucivorus*

The wart-biter is a long-horned grasshopper or bush-cricket, slightly less than an inch and a half long. It has large, powerful jaws and its curious name is based on the superstition that in the past Swedish peasants used it to bite off their warts.

The adults are found in August and September, but are only active on hot days. The species is not very particular about its habitat but seems to prefer chalk grassland and heaths, with long, rank herbage.

It occurs in seven or eight widely-scattered localities in Southern England, and also in Europe. Where turf is kept short, thus benefiting other species, the wart-biter suffers.

It is protected in one National Nature Reserve.

Field cricket   *Gryllus campestris*

The field cricket is one of the Gryllidae family, or true crickets. It has only vestigial wings and cannot fly. Like all crickets it has long antennae, but unlike most of its kind it prefers the sunshine and is active by day. Its hearing organs are on its front legs.

The shrill 'song' of the male field cricket can be heard continuously from May to August, when the adults reach the end of their short life. Though rather repetitive, the song is very pleasant, and in Southern Europe field crickets are kept as domestic pets.

The species thrives on grassland in sandy areas. Once quite widespread, it is now thought to be confined to two sites in Southern England, though attempts have been made to introduce it in other suitable sites. Its scarcity is mainly due to the conversion of heath grassland for farming and forestry.

Mole cricket   *Gryllotalpa gryllotalpu*

The mole cricket is one of the largest British insects, with a robust body nearly one and a half inches long. Its powerful front legs are well adapted for digging, and like its namesake it spends much of its time tunnelling underground. The female makes a nest and, unusually for an insect, guards her eggs and her young for their first two or three weeks of life.

The mole cricket lives in damp meadows in river valleys, taking to the air in clumsy flight on warm summer evenings.

Though it is widespread in Europe, in England it seems to be confined to the south.

Its exact status is unknown, though it appears to be rare. Its preferred habitat is limited, and vulnerable to change.

Carthusian snail _Monacha cartusiana_

The carthusian snail is one of the Helicidae, the most successful family of European snails. About ⁵⁄₁₆ inch in height and ½ to ⅝ inch broad, it lives in chalk grassland and sand dunes in South-East England.

Like all snails it is a hermaphrodite, and it belongs to a group which sometimes forms chains when copulating. There is a 'male' at one end and a 'female' at the other, with the snails between acting as both male and female. It is also found in the Mediterranean regions of Europe.

Glutinous snail _Myxas glutinosa_

The glutinous snail is a pond snail belonging to the family Lymnaeidae. It is about half an inch in height and slightly less in breadth. Its shell is thin, almost transparent, and very fragile – as can be seen from these museum specimens.

It frequents lakes and sluggish rivers, mostly in upland areas. It has been recorded at locations from Southern England to Yorkshire, and is also found in Ireland, Europe, and eastwards to Siberia. It now seems to be very scarce in Britain, and there have been no recent reports of its existence.

Sandbowl snail _Catinella arenaria_

The sandbowl snail belongs to the widespread Succineidae family. It is very similar to one of the closely-related amber snails, and can only be identified reliably by dissection. About a quarter of an inch in height, it has difficulty in withdrawing its somewhat ungainly body into its thick, rather rudimentary shell.

It lives in damp, sparsely-vegetated places among sand dunes, and in marshes. There is one large and flourishing colony in a National Nature Reserve in the west of England. The species is also found in a few places in Europe.

Notes on The Wildlife and Countryside Act 1981

This legislation began its existence in the House of Lords on 25 November 1980, and after passing through both Houses of Parliament finally became law on 30 October 1981. Apart from the need to improve protection for our wild animals and plants, the Act was necessary in order to comply with certain international agreements (especially the Convention on the Conservation of European Wildlife and Natural Habitats, often known as the Berne Convention, and the EEC Directive on the Conservation of Wild Birds) which Britain had already ratified.

During the Act's passage through Parliament, debate was prolonged and sometimes heated, and what eventually emerged was a complex piece of legislation dealing with a wide variety of subjects. The following is a summary of the main provisions of the Act.

In general all wild plants are protected to some degree, and all wild birds are protected unless otherwise stated. Other animals, however, are not protected unless specifically mentioned in the Act or covered by some other legislation.

Three cetaceans (common and bottle-nosed dolphin and common porpoise) are given full protection, although they are not particularly threatened in British waters; the white-beaked, white-sided, and Risso's dolphins are all probably more vulnerable. The reason for singling out the first three of these species for protection was their listing as 'strictly protected' in the Berne Convention. The inclusion of species such as the shrew, dormouse, hedgehog, wild cat, pine marten and polecat in Schedule 6 (prohibition of certain methods of killing) also stemmed from their protection under the Berne Convention. The reason why the wild cat, pine marten, and polecat are not given *full protection*, however, is that all three are making a recovery from 19th-century persecution and seem to be expanding their ranges in this country. Though the population of the dormouse appears to have diminished since Victorian and Edwardian times it still has the same distribution (basically in Southern and Central England and Wales) as in the past, and therefore was not given full protection.

While the badger is now almost fully protected, its sett is not, unlike the holt of the otter or the roosting sites of bats. It derives its protection under the Badgers Act, rather than being included in Schedule 5 of the Wildlife and Countryside Act. As it is still widespread and numerous, protection is more a question of animal welfare than conservation.

A small number of invertebrates are protected under the Act, but many more are threatened. However, the principle is now established that creatures such as snails, spiders, and beetles are worthy of protection, and others can always be added to the list if a particular threat arises.

Note Where fines are mentioned in the following summary they apply to a *single* offence. When the offence involves more than one bird, egg, plant, etc, each is liable to incur a separate fine.

Birds

The basic principle is that all wild birds are protected throughout the year, unless otherwise stated. This means that, with certain exceptions, you may not kill, injure, or take any wild bird. Protection is also extended to nests (while in use or being built) and to eggs.

Schedule 1 – Part 1

The following birds are fully protected by special penalties at all times. As well as the general provisions mentioned above, it is an offence to disturb intentionally any bird listed in Schedule 1 while it is building a nest, or on or near a nest containing eggs or young, or to disturb the young of these birds. Fifty-seven of the birds listed below are shown in the illustrated section of this book.

Avocet	Chough
Bee-eater	Corncrake
Bittern	Spotted crake
Little bittern	Crossbills (all
Bluethroat	species)
Brambling	Stone curlew
Cirl bunting	Divers (all species)
Lapland bunting	Dotterel
Snow bunting	Long-tailed duck
Honey buzzard	Golden eagle

White-tailed eagle
Gyr falcon
Fieldfare
Firecrest
Garganey
Black-tailed godwit
Goshawk
Black-necked grebe
Slavonian grebe
Greenshank
Little gull
Mediterranean gull
Harriers (all species)
Purple heron
Hobby
Hoopoe
Kingfisher
Red kite
Merlin
Golden oriole
Osprey
Barn owl
Snowy owl
Peregrine
Leach's petrel
Red-necked
    phalarope
Kentish plover
Little ringed plover
Common quail
Black redstart

Redwing
Scarlet rosefinch
Ruff
Green sandpiper
Purple sandpiper
Wood sandpiper
Scaup
Common scoter
Velvet scoter
Serin
Shorelark
Red-backed shrike
Spoonbill
Black-winged stilt
Temminck's stint
Bewick's swan
Whooper swan
Black tern
Little tern
Roseate tern
Bearded tit
Crested tit
Short-toed
    treecreeper
Cetti's warbler
Dartford warbler
Marsh warbler
Savi's warbler
Whimbrel
Woodlark
Wryneck

Schedule 1 – Part 2

The following birds are protected by special penalties during the close season only (1 February to 31 August; or 21 February to 31 August below high water mark). Outside this period they may be taken or killed. The goldeneye and pintail are shown in the illustrated section of this book.

Goldeneye
Greylag goose (only in Outer Hebrides, Caithness, Sutherland and Wester Ross)
Pintail

Schedule 2 – Part 1

The following birds are protected during the close season only (1 February to 31 August; or 21 February to 31 August for ducks and geese when below the high water mark). Outside this period they may be taken or killed.

Capercaillie (close
    season is
    1 February to
    30 September)
Coot
Tufted duck
Gadwall
Goldeneye
Canada goose

Greylag goose
Pink-footed goose
White-fronted goose
    (in England and
    Wales only. In
    Scotland it is
    protected outside
    the close season.)
Mallard

Moorhen
Pintail
Golden plover
Pochard
Shoveler
Common snipe
    (close season is
    1 February to
    11 August)
Teal

Wigeon
Woodcock (close
    season is 1
    February to 30
    September, except
    in Scotland,
    where it is 1
    February to 31
    August.)

Schedule 2 – Part 2

The following birds are considered pest species and may be taken or killed by authorised persons (e.g. landowners or occupiers) at all times.

Crow
Collared dove
Great black-backed
    gull
Lesser black-backed
    gull
Herring gull
Jackdaw

Jay
Magpie
Feral pigeon
Rook
House sparrow
Starling
Woodpigeon

Schedule 3 – Part 1

The following birds may be sold alive at all times, if ringed and bred in captivity.

Blackbird
Brambling
Bullfinch
Reed bunting
Chaffinch
Dunnock
Goldfinch
Greenfinch
Jackdaw
Jay

Linnet
Magpie
Barn owl
Redpoll
Siskin
Starling
Song thrush
Twite
Yellowhammer

Schedule 3 – Part 2

The following birds may be sold dead at all times.

Feral pigeon
Woodpigeon

Schedule 3 – Part 3

The following birds may be sold dead from 1 September to 28 February.

Capercaillie
Coot
Tufted duck
Mallard
Pintail
Golden plover

Pochard
Shoveler
Common snipe
Teal
Wigeon
Woodcock

Schedule 4

A number of birds must be registered and ringed if kept in captivity. This list is essentially the same as Schedule 1 – Part 1, with the following exceptions.

Brambling
Garganey

Little gull
Mediterranean gull

Purple heron   Scaup
Barn owl   Bewick's swan
Snowy owl   Whooper swan

In addition, all birds of prey in the world are included on the list, except for Old World vultures. Address for registration: Department of the Environment, Wildlife Licensing Section, Tollgate House, Houlton Street, Bristol, BS2 9DJ.

SALE OF LIVE WILD BIRDS AND THEIR EGGS
It is an offence to sell any live wild bird except where provided for in Schedule 3 – Part 1. It is also an offence to sell the egg of any wild bird (whether or not taken in contravention of the Act).

SALE OF DEAD WILD BIRDS
It is an offence to sell any dead wild bird (including its skin or any other part) unless listed in Schedule 3 – Parts 2 and 3. Game birds may be sold dead only during the open season and for 10 days immediately after the end of that season.

EXHIBITION OF WILD BIRDS
It is an offence to exhibit any live wild bird at a competition except where provided for in Schedule 3 – Part 1.

METHODS OF KILLING AND TAKING BIRDS
Certain methods of killing, injuring, or taking birds are prohibited. These include gins, springes, traps (e.g. pole traps), snares, nets, bird lime, electrical scaring devices, poisonous or stupefying substances, bows, automatic or semi-automatic weapons, and night-shooting devices. The use of live birds as decoys, whether tethered, blinded, or maimed, is also illegal.

PHOTOGRAPHY
Birds listed on Schedule 1 may not be photographed at the nest without a licence.

GAME BIRDS
Game birds are not included in the Wildlife and Countryside Act, but they are fully protected during the close season under the Game Acts, as follows:
Pheasant (close season 2 February to 30 September)
Partridge (2 February to 31 August)
Black grouse (11 December to 19 August)
Red grouse (11 December to 11 August)
Ptarmigan, in Scotland (11 December to 11 August)

EXCEPTIONS AND LICENCES
The provisions of the Act concerning wild birds are complicated, and there are a number of exceptions to the provisions as outlined above. For example, certain actions may not be illegal if they are 'the incidental result of a lawful operation and could not reasonably have been avoided'. Licences may also be issued for taking, killing or disturbing wild birds for a number of purposes, such as falconry, taxidermy, photography of Schedule 1 species, preventing serious damage to livestock or crops, and for scientific or educational purposes.

FINES
The maximum fine for offences involving a single bird, egg, or nest is £200. For offences involving a Schedule 1 species, or an illegal method of killing, the maximum fine is £1,000.

Other animals
A total of 52 other animals receive special protection under Schedule 5 of the Act. All 52 species are featured in the illustrated section of this book. Forty-four species are protected at all times, but 8 are protected in respect of trade only.

Specially protected wild animals
The following animals are specially protected under Schedule 5 of the Act. It is an offence to kill, injure, take, possess, or sell any of them; or to damage, destroy, or obstruct access to any place which they use for shelter, protection, or breeding, or to disturb them while they are there.

Bats (all 15 species)   Black veined moth
Otter   Essex emerald moth
Red squirrel   New forest burnet
Bottle-nosed dolphin   moth
Common dolphin   Reddish buff moth
Common porpoise   Field cricket
Sand lizard   Mole cricket
Smooth snake   Norfolk aeshna
Great crested newt   dragonfly
Natterjack toad   Rainbow leaf beetle
Burbot   Wart-biter
Chequered skipper   grasshopper
   butterfly   Fen raft spider
Heath fritillary   Ladybird spider
   butterfly   Carthusian snail
Large blue butterfly   Glutinous snail
Swallowtail butterfly   Sandbowl snail
Barberry carpet
   moth

Other protected species
The following species are protected in respect of trade under Schedule 5 of the Act, and may not be offered for sale without a licence. ('Sale' includes hire, barter and exchange.)
Palmate newt   Smooth newt

Common frog	Slow-worm
Common toad	Grass snake
Viviparous lizard	Adder

Bats

Bats receive fuller protection than other animals because of their special roosting requirements. The provisions relating to their places of shelter, breeding, etc, are therefore extended even to houses and outbuildings. The Nature Conservancy Council must be informed of any proposed action to get rid of bats, or any operation (including wood treatment) likely to disturb them or their roosts. The NCC should be allowed time to advise on whether the operation should be carried out and, if it is permissible, on the method to be used and its timing. The only exception is for bats in the living area of a house.

Cetaceans

In addition to the two dolphins and one porpoise listed above, all whales, dolphins, and porpoises (as well as sturgeons) in British waters are also protected, as, whether dead or alive, they are considered Royal Fish and belong to the Crown. The liability for disposal or burial of carcases belonging to the Crown rests with the Department of Trade.

PHOTOGRAPHY
Animals receiving special protection must not be photographed in their places of shelter, breeding, etc., without a licence.

EXCEPTIONS AND LICENCES
As with birds, there are a number of exceptions to the general provisions mentioned here, and licences may be issued for certain actions or operations.

FINES
The maximum fine for offences involving animals listed on Schedule 5 is £1000.

METHODS OF KILLING OR TAKING WILD ANIMALS
The Act prohibits self-locking snares, bows, crossbows, and explosives (other than firearm ammunition), for the purpose of killing or taking any wild animal. In addition, the use of live mammals or birds as decoys for the purpose of killing or taking wild animals is prohibited.

Schedule 6

The following animals listed in Schedule 6 may not (in addition to the methods of killing listed above) be killed or taken by any kind of trap or snare, electrical stunning device, poisonous or stupefying substance, net, automatic or semi-automatic weapon; device or artificial light for dazzling, illuminating a target, or for night-shooting; sound recording used as a decoy; or any mechanically propelled vehicle in immediate pursuit of such an animal. The effect of these prohibitions is that the listed species may only be legally killed or taken by shooting (with a non-automatic weapon).

Badger	Pine marten
Bats (all species)	Otter
Wild cat	Polecat
Bottle-nosed dolphin	Common porpoise
Common dolphin	Shrews (all species)
Dormice (all species)	Red squirrel
Hedgehog	

FINES
The maximum fine for offences involving animals listed in Schedule 6 is £1000.

Hares, rabbit, badger, deer, and seals

The Act makes certain amendments to other Acts affecting these animals. From a conservation point of view the most significant amendment is the prohibition of landowners or occupiers from killing badgers on their own land without a licence. This effectively gives the badger similar protection to animals listed in Schedule 5.

Plants

It is illegal to uproot any wild plant intentionally, except on your own land or with permission from the owner or occupier. It is not illegal to pick most wild flowers or fruit (such as blackberries), though there may be byelaws making this illegal in Nature Reserves.

The Act names 62 plants which receive special protection. All of them except one species of sea lavender are shown in the illustrated section of this book. It is an offence to intentionally pick, uproot, or destroy any of these species, or even to collect their flowers or seeds. It is also an offence to sell these plants or their seeds if taken from the wild.

Small alison	Diapensia
Bedstraw broomrape	Field eryngo
	Dickie's bladder fern
Oxtongue broomrape	Killarney fern
	Brown galingale
Thistle broomrape	Alpine gentian
Wood calamint	Spring gentian
Alpine catchfly	Water germander
Rock cinquefoil	Wild gladiolus
Triangular club-rush	Sickle-leaved hare's-ear
Wild cotoneaster	
Field cow-wheat	Small hare's-ear
Jersey cudweed	Blue heath

Red helleborine
Perennial knawel
Sea knotgrass
Sea lavender (2 spp.)
Round-headed leek
Least lettuce
Snowdon lily
Rough
　marsh-mallow
Early spider orchid
Fen orchid
Ghost orchid
Lady's slipper
Late spider orchid
Lizard orchid
Military orchid
Monkey orchid
Plymouth pear
Cheddar pink
Childling pink
Norwegian
　sandwort

Teesdale sandwort
Drooping saxifrage
Tufted saxifrage
Whorled
　Solomon's-seal
Alpine sow-thistle
Adder's-tongue
　spearwort
Spiked speedwell
Purple spurge
Starfruit
Fen violet
Ribbon-leaved
　water-plantain
Starved wood-sedge
Alpine woodsia
Oblong woodsia
Field wormwood
Downy woundwort
Limestone
　woundwort
Greater yellow-rattle

EXCEPTIONS AND LICENCES

As with birds and other animals, there are a number of exceptions, and licences may be issued for certain purposes (e.g. to collect seed for conservation reasons).

FINES

The maximum fine for offences involving plants is £500.

Introduced species of animals and plants

It is illegal to release or allow to escape into the wild any animal 'which is not ordinarily resident in and is not a regular visitor to Great Britain in a wild state', or any of the species listed below which are already established in the wild. This does not cover certain animals which, though originally introduced from elsewhere, are now accepted as part of the British fauna. Under this section of the Act, zoos are responsible for ensuring that their animals do not escape into the wild. It is also illegal to plant or otherwise cause to grow in the wild certain species of plants.

Schedule 9 – Part 1

Prohibited animal introductions

Large-mouthed
　black bass
Rock bass
Bitterling
Budgerigar
Capercaillie

Coypu
Fat dormouse
Carolina wood duck
Mandarin duck
Ruddy duck
White-tailed eagle

Edible frog
European or
　common tree frog
Marsh frog
Mongolian gerbil
Canada goose
Egyptian goose
Night heron
Common wall lizard
Prairie marmot, or
　prairie dog
American mink
Alpine newt
Ring-necked
　parakeet
Chukar partridge
Rock partridge
Golden pheasant
Lady Amherst's
　pheasant

Reeves' pheasant
Silver pheasant
Crested porcupine
Himalayan
　porcupine
Pumpkinseed (or
　sun-fish or
　pond-perch)
Bobwhite quail
Black rat
Grey squirrel
European pond
　terrapin
African clawed toad
Midwife toad
Yellow-bellied toad
Red-necked wallaby
Wels (European
　catfish)
Zander

Schedule 9 – Part 2

Prohibited plant introductions

Giant hogweed
Giant kelp
Japanese knotweed
Japanese seaweed

EXCEPTIONS AND LICENCES

There are no exceptions, though it may be a defence that the accused 'took all reasonable steps and exercised all due diligence to avoid committing the offence'. Nevertheless, licences may be issued to introduce these species.

FINES

An offence under this section of the Act may attract an unlimited fine, up to the statutory maximum.

Other provisions

Parts II and III of the Act deal in some detail with various measures to conserve and protect the countryside, in particular with regard to Sites of Special Scientific Interest, National Parks, and Public Rights of Way.

For the first time, provision is made for the establishment of Marine Nature Reserves.

Further information

This summary of the provisions of the Wildlife and Countryside Act 1981 should be used for guidance only, and should not be taken as being definitive. Further guidance can be obtained in the publications listed below:

Wildlife, the Law and You (single copies 50p incl. p&p)

Focus on Bats (single copies 65p incl. p&p)
Available from the Nature Conservancy Council, Attingham Park, Shrewsbury, Salop, SY4 4TW.

Wildlife and the Law – No. 1: Wild Plants
Wildlife and the Law – No. 2: Reptiles and Amphibians
Code of Conduct for the Conservation of Wild Plants
Single copies available free of charge, on receipt of a 9″ × 6″ stamped addressed envelope, from the Council for Environmental Conservation (CoEnCo), c/o Zoological Society of London, Regent's Park, London NW1 4RY.

Information about Birds and the Law
Bird Photography and the Law
(A new edition of the booklet *Wild Birds and the Law* is in preparation.)
Single copies available free of charge, on receipt of a 9″ × 6″ stamped addressed envelope, from the Royal Society for the Protection of Birds, The Lodge, Sandy, Bedfordshire, SG19 2DL.

For complete information, consult the Act itself. Copies are available from HMSO, PO Box 569, London SE1 9NH at £7.05 (incl. p&p), or through any bookseller.

Natural history and conservation organisations

The following list is by no means comprehensive but includes most of the major and national organisations. It is based on information from a variety of sources, in particular *Environmental Education – Sources of Information 1981*, prepared by the Department of Education and Science and the Central Office of Information, and the *Directory of Natural History and Related Societies in Britain and Ireland*, published by the British Museum (Natural History), Cromwell Road, London, SW7 5BD, at £15.00. The latter is an invaluable compilation listing some 750 societies, especially local groups and those devoted to specialised interests.

Amateur Entomologists' Society
355 Hounslow Road, Hanworth, Feltham, Middlesex, TW13 5JH/tel: 01–894 9001
Encourages the study of insects with publications, correspondence, meetings, and exhibitions. Holds field meetings for conservation studies. Activities orientated towards amateurs and beginners.

Association for the Protection of Rural Scotland
20 Falkland Avenue, Newton Mearns, G77 5DR/tel: 041 639 2069
Aims to protect the Scottish countryside from unreasonable or unacceptable development. Advice and information given on matters affecting the general welfare of rural areas.

Association for the Study of Reptilia and Amphibia
The ASRA Rooms, Cotswold Wildlife Park, Burford, Oxfordshire, OX8 4JW
Main aim is to stimulate public interest in reptiles and amphibians and to dispel the unfavourable attitudes often directed towards these animals. Holds monthly meetings. Provides an information service. Supports reptile conservation projects.

Botanical Society of Edinburgh
c/o Botany Department, University of Edinburgh, Mayfield Road, Edinburgh, EH9 3JH
Scotland's national botanical society, which aims to promote the study of botany, the acquisition of knowledge and the appreciation of Scottish flora. Holds regular indoor and field meetings in several Scottish towns and cities.

Botanical Society of the British Isles (BSBI)
c/o Department of Botany, British Museum (Natural History), Cromwell Road, London, SW7 5BD/tel: 01–589 6323
The country's leading botanical society, open to amateurs and professionals. Specialises in the study of flowering plants and ferns. Holds field meetings in various parts of the country, study weekends, conferences, and exhibitions.

British Association of Nature Conservationists (BANC)
Rectory Farm, Stanton St John, Oxfordshire, OX9 1HF
Promotes the better application of ecology to the practical issues of nature conservation and provides a forum for the exchange of views on all aspects of conservation.

British Butterfly Conservation Society
Tudor House, 102 Chaveney Road, Quorn, Loughborough, Leicestershire, LE12 8AD/tel: 0509 42870
Aims to protect all species of British butterflies by conserving them in the wild or by breeding them in captivity and releasing them in their natural habitats. Holds field meetings.

British Deer Society
The Mill House, Bishopstrow, Warminster, Wiltshire/tel: 0985 216608

Concerned with all aspects of the relation of deer to man and his environment, including conservation and humane methods of management and control. Holds educational courses and outdoor meetings.

British Dragonfly Society
48 Somersby Avenue, Watton, Derbyshire, S42 7LY
A newly formed society for anyone interested in dragonflies.

British Ecological Society
Harvest House, 62 London Road, Reading, RG1 5AS/tel: 0734 861345
Promotes the understanding of ecology as a scientific discipline. Publishes three journals and holds a number of meetings, including an annual field meeting and an annual symposium.

British Herpetological Society
c/o Zoological Society of London, Regent's Park, London, NW1 4RY/tel: 01–722 3333
Promotes the study of herpetology, with special reference to British reptiles and amphibians, and with emphasis on conservation and captive breeding. Holds eight meetings a year in London.

British Mountaineering Council
Crawford House, Booth Street East, Manchester, M13 9RZ
Though mainly concerned with mountaineering as a sport, also promotes the conservation of mountain areas and cliff faces.

British Mycological Society
c/o Department of Plant Sciences, Wye College (University of London), Wye, Near Ashford, Kent, TN25 5AH/tel: 0233 812401 ext. 237
Promotes the study of all aspects of fungi. Holds courses, conferences, and meetings.

British Naturalists' Association
Auquhorthies, 2a London Road, Thatcham, Berkshire, RG13 4LP
Promotes communication between amateur naturalists in different parts of the country through its publications and a number of local groups and affiliated societies. Holds field meetings and lectures.

British Sub-Aqua Club
70 Brompton Road, London, SW3 1HA/tel: 01–584 7163/4
Though mainly concerned with the promotion of underwater exploration, science, and sport, the club is involved in conservation of underwater resources. Many branches, meetings and activities around the country.

British Trust for Conservation Volunteers (BTCV)
10–14 Duke Street, Reading, Berkshire, RG1 4RU/tel: 0734 596171
Promotes practical conservation work by volunteers (between 16 and 70). Tasks may occupy a day, a weekend, or longer. Publishes a series of practical conservation handbooks, e.g. *Hedging, Dry Stone Walling*, etc. Several regional branches.

British Trust for Ornithology (BTO)
Beech Grove, Station Road, Tring, Hertfordshire, HP23 5NR/tel: 044282 3461
Encourages and organises amateur study and field research in ornithology, and runs the national Bird Ringing scheme, the largest and technically most advanced in Europe. Passes on its research findings to other bodies, including conservation societies, for action. About 70 regional representatives.

Commons, Open Spaces, and Footpaths Preservation Society
25a Bell Street, Henley-on-Thames, Oxfordshire
Promotes the protection of commons, village greens, and other open spaces, and the preservation of public rights of way.

Conchological Society of Great Britain and Ireland
51 Wychwood Avenue, Luton, Bedfordshire, LU2 7HT/tel: 0582 24801

Encourages the study of molluscs – marine, non-marine, and terrestrial – in Britain and throughout the world. Holds field meetings and winter indoor meetings in London.

Conservation Society
12a Guildford Street, Chertsey, Surrey, KT16 9BQ
Concerned with population growth and the use of natural resources. Promotes policies designed to reduce the rapid depletion of resources and environmental degradation.

Council for the Protection of Rural England (CPRE)
4 Hobart Place, London, SW1W 0HY/tel: 01–235 9481
Organises action to improve, protect, and preserve the rural scenery and amenities of the countryside, and acts as a centre for giving or obtaining advice and information. Participates in public enquiries and arranges conferences. Many regional branches.

Council for the Protection of Rural Wales (CPRW)
(Cymdeithas Diogelu Harddwch Cymru)
14 Broad Street, Welshpool, Powys, SY21 7SD/tel: 0938 2525
Aims similar to the CPRE above.

Farming and Wildlife Advisory Group (FWAG)
c/o The Lodge, Sandy, Bedfordshire, SG19 2DL/tel: 0767 80551
Promotes understanding by farmers and conservationists of each other's problems and points of view, and shows how the requirements of agriculture, landscape, and wildlife can be reconciled. Many county groups, which organise exhibitions, farm walks, and other events.

Fauna and Flora Preservation Society (FFPS)
c/o Zoological Society of London, Regent's Park, London, NW1 4RY/tel: 01–586 0872
Works to protect endangered wildlife throughout the world. Publishes informative journal *Oryx* dealing with worldwide conservation issues and holds several meetings a year in London.

Field Studies Council
Preston Montford, Montford Bridge, Shrewsbury, Salop, SY4 1HW/tel: 0743 850674
Promotes understanding of the environment through residential courses in a wide variety of subjects, ranging from natural history through geology to archaeology. Field centres are located in Wales and in England from Devon to Yorkshire.

Friends of the Earth (FOE)
377 City Road, London, EC1/tel: 01–837 0731
Environmental pressure group that campaigns on issues such as natural resource depletion, transport, safer energy, and wildlife and the countryside. Has recently launched a UK Countryside Action Campaign. Works through about 250 local groups.

Geologists' Association
Burlington House, Piccadilly, London, W1U 0JU/tel: 01–734 1040
Fosters an interest in geology as a hobby, through lectures, field trips, and the publication of papers and field guides. Several local groups.

Hawk Trust
c/o Birds of Prey Section, Zoological Society of London, Regent's Park, London, NW1 4RY
Encourages the conservation and appreciation of birds of prey, especially the British species. Initiates research on the more threatened species and helps field conservation by providing voluntary wardens at vulnerable nesting sites.

London Wildlife Trust
1 Thorpe Close, London, W10 5XL/tel: 01–968 5368
Campaigns to encourage an interest in the conservation of the wildlife of the GLC area. Manages nature reserves and creates new sites for wildlife from the inner city to the outer suburbs. Equivalent to the Nature Conservation Trusts which are affiliated to the Royal Society for Nature Conservation.

Mammal Society
Burlington House, Piccadilly, London, W1V 0LQ/tel: 01–734 1040
Promotes the study of mammals, primarily in Britain. Venues of annual meetings vary. Specialist groups within the society cover bats, carnivores, cetaceans, etc. Various publications include an excellent and informative newsletter. Active youth group organises field trips.

Men of the Trees
Crawley Down, Crawley, Sussex, RH10 4HL/tel: 0243 712536
Encourages an appreciation of the value of tree-cover and the planting and protection of trees. Branches hold regular meetings. Professional advisory service available.

National Trust
42 Queen Anne's Gate, London, SW1H 9AS/tel: 01–222 9251
Works for the permanent preservation of land and buildings of historic interest and natural beauty. Largest private landowner in Britain controlling many estates, hundreds of miles of coastline, and large areas of downland, moorland, woodland, and farmland. Many local groups and camps for young people.

National Trust for Scotland
5 Charlotte Square, Edinburgh, EH2 4DU/tel: 031 226 5922
Aims and activities are similar to those of the National Trust (see above).

Nature Conservancy Council (NCC)
19–20 Belgrave Square, London, SW1X 8PY/tel: 01–235 3241
The government body, financed through the Department of the Environment, that promotes nature conservation in Britain. Advises the government, local authorities, and the public at large, about conservation. Establishes and manages the network of nearly 200 National Nature Reserves and selects and notifies Sites of Special Scientific Interest to landowners and the relevant authorities. All activities are based on detailed ecological research and survey. Publishes a wide range of excellent leaflets, booklets, and other educational material. Catalogue of publications available from Interpretive Branch, Nature Conservancy Council, Attingham Park, Shrewsbury, Salop, SY4 4TW.

Otter Trust
Earsham, Bungay, Suffolk
Promotes the conservation of otters, including captive breeding and eventual re-introduction, and the establishment of otter havens.

Ramblers' Association
1–5 Wandsworth Road, London, SW8 2LJ
Objects include promoting care of the countryside, preservation of natural beauty, protection of footpaths, and provision of access to the countryside. Occasional conferences.

Royal Society for Nature Conservation (RSNC)
The Green, Nettleham, Lincolnshire, LN2 2NR/tel: 0522 752326
Promotes nature conservation at all levels, and the establishment and management of nature reserves. Makes representation to government on legislation and matters affecting the environment. Is the national association for 44 mostly county-based Nature Conservation Trusts (addresses available on application), which own or manage some 1,400 nature reserves. Joining one of these Trusts is the prime way of becoming involved in conservation at the local level. Runs the Watch Club for young people.

Royal Society for the Prevention of Cruelty to Animals (RSPCA)
Causeway, Horsham, West Sussex, RH12 1HG
Though mainly concerned with animal welfare, the RSPCA also includes wildlife conservation among its aims (especially where cruelty might be involved).

Royal Society for the Protection of Birds (RSPB)
The Lodge, Sandy, Bedfordshire, SG19 2DL/tel: 0767 80551
Works for the conservation and protection of wild birds, especially rare species. Owns, leases, or manages some 80 nature reserves, many of them quite large. Carries out scientific

research, and is active in the enforcement of conservation laws, education, publishing, and film production. Over 200 local branches. Largest membership of any society in the British voluntary conservation movement. Runs the Young Ornithologists' Club for young people aged 9–16.

Underwater Conservation Society
NCC, Godwin House, George Street, Huntingdon, Cambridgeshire, PE18 6BU
Promotes the study and protection of the natural and historical features of the underwater environment. Holds regional meetings.

Wild Flower Society
Harvest House, 62 London Road, Reading, Berkshire, RG1 5AS/tel: 0734 861345
Encourages an interest in and thus a greater knowledge of wild flowers among children and adults, and promotes education related to the conservation of wild flowers and the countryside.

Wildfowl Trust
Slimbridge, Gloucestershire, GL2 7BT/tel: 045389 333
Conducts scientific research into wildfowl in the wild and in captivity. Activities include breeding wildfowl, especially endangered species, education of the public, and involvement in conservation. Maintains splendid collections of captive wildfowl at Slimbridge, and at other centres in Lancashire, Cambridgeshire, Tyne and Wear, Sussex, and Dumfriesshire.

Woodland Trust
Westgate, Grantham, Lincolnshire, NG31 6LL/tel: 0476 74297
Protects – through ownership – areas of native British broadleaved woodland. Also establishes new woodland by planting trees. Protected areas number over 100, ranging from a few trees to hundreds of acres.

World Wildlife Fund-UK (WWF)
11–13 Ockford Road, Godalming, Surrey, GU7 1QU/tel: 04868 20551
The British branch of an international organisation which raises money for conservation projects designed to ensure the wise use of renewable natural resources, including wild animals, plants, and their habitats. Provides very substantial funds for projects in Britain, especially for land purchase (for nature reserves), but also for scientific research into threatened species, education, and support of other organisations, notably the British Trust for Conservation Volunteers.

Young People's Trust for Endangered Species
19 Quarry Street, Guildford, Surrey/tel: 0483 39600
Encourages a wider interest in the conservation of nature and natural resources, especially endangered species, at home and abroad. Works through schools and youth groups, offering a programme of school lectures, field courses, and summer camps.

Young Zoologists' Club (XYZ Club)
c/o Zoological Society of London, Regent's Park, London, NW1 4RY/tel: 01–722 3333
Encourages young people (aged 9–18) to develop an interest in animal biology. Meetings held at the Zoological Society's zoos at Regent's Park (London) and Whipsnade (Bedfordshire).

Bibliography

Arnold, E. N. and Burton, J. A. *Field Guide to the Reptiles and Amphibians of Britain and Europe*. Collins, London, 1978.

Baker, M. *Discovering the Folklore of Plants*. Shire, Aylesbury, 1980.

Blamey, M. *Flowers of the Countryside*. Collins, London, 1980.

Body, R. *Agriculture: The Triumph and the Shame*. Temple Smith, London, 1983.

Book of British Birds. Drive Publications, London, 1969.

Boyle, C. L. (Ed.) *RSPCA Book of British Mammals*. Collins, London, 1981.

Bristowe, W. S. *The World of Spiders*. Collins, London, 1958.

Burton, J. *The Oxford Book of Insects*. Oxford University Press, 1979.

Chinery, M. *A Field Guide to the Insects of Britain and Northern Europe*. Collins, London, 1976.

Clapham, A. R., Tutin, T. G. and Warburg, E. F. *Flora of the British Isles*. Cambridge University Press, 1962.

Conservation and Development Programme for the UK, The. Kogan Page, London, 1983.

Corbet, G. B. and Southern, H. N. (Eds.) *The Handbook of British Mammals*. Blackwell, Oxford, 1977.

Dony, J. G., Rob, C. M. and Perring, F. H. *English Names of Wild Flowers*. Butterworth, London, 1974.

Ellis, A. E. *British Snails*. Oxford University Press, 1969.

Ellis, E. A., Perring, F. H. and Randall, R. E. *Britain's Rarest Plants*. Jarrold, Norwich, 1977.

Evans, P. G. H. 'Cetaceans in British Waters' in *Mammal Review*, Vol. 10, No. 1, Blackwell, Oxford, 1980.

Field Guide to the Birds of Britain. Reader's Digest, London, 1981.

Field Guide to the Wild Flowers of Britain. Reader's Digest, London, 1981.

Fitter, R., Fitter, A. and Blamey, M. *The Wild Flowers of Britain and Northern Europe*. Collins, London, 1974.

Fitter, R. and M. *Penguin Dictionary of British Natural History*. Penguin, Harmondsworth, 1978.

Fraser, F. C. *British Whales, Dolphins and Porpoises*. British Museum (Natural History), London, 1976.

Frazer, D. *Reptiles and Amphibians in Britain*. Collins, London, 1983.

Freethy, R. *The Making of the British Countryside*. David & Charles, Newton Abbot, 1981.

Gilmour, J. and Walters, M. *Wild Flowers*. Collins, London, 1973.

Gooden, R. *British Butterflies*. David & Charles, Newton Abbot, 1978.

Gooders, J. *Collins British Birds*. Collins, London, 1982.

Greenoak, F. *All the Birds of the Air*. Deutsch, London, 1979.

Heinzel, H., Fitter, R. and Parslow, J. *The Birds of Britain and Europe*. Collins, London, 1979.

Higgins, L. G. and Riley, N. D. *A Field Guide to the Butterflies of Britain and Europe*. Collins, London, 1980.

Kerney, M. P. and Cameron, R. A. D. *A Field Guide to the Land Snails of Britain and North-West Europe*. Collins, London, 1979.

Lousley, J. E. *Wild Flowers of Chalk and Limestone*. Collins, London, 1969.

Mabey, R. *The Common Ground*. Hutchinson, London, 1980.

Matthews, L. H. *Mammals in the British Isles*. Collins, London, 1982.

Morris, P. (Consultant Ed.) *The Country Life Book of the Natural History of the British Isles*. Country Life Books, London, 1979.

Muus, B. J. and Dahlstrom, P. *Freshwater Fishes of Britain and Europe*. Collins, London, 1978.

Nature Conservancy Council's *Eighth Report* (April 1 1981 – March 31 1982). Nature Conservancy Council, London, 1983.

Newman, L. H. *The Complete British Butterflies in Colour*. Michael Joseph, London, 1968.

Parslow, J. *Breeding Birds of Britain and Ireland*. Poyser, Berkhamsted, 1973.

Perring, F. H. (Ed.) *The Flora of a Changing Britain*. Botanical Society of the British Isles Conference Report No. 11. Classey, Hampton, Middlesex, 1970.

Perring, F. H. and Farrell, L. *British Red Data Book 1: Vascular Plants*. Royal Society for Nature Conservation, Lincoln, 1983.

Perring, F. H. and Randall, R. E. *Britain's Endangered Plants*. Jarrold, Norwich, 1981.

Peterson, R. T. *A Field Guide to the Birds East of the Rockies*. Houghton Mifflin, Boston, USA, 1980.

Peterson, R. T., Mountfort, G. and Hollom, P. A. D. *A Field Guide to the Birds of Britain and Europe*. Collins, London, 1983.

Potterton, D. (Ed.) *Culpeper's Colour Herbal*. Foulsham, London, 1983.

Pratt, A. *The Flowering Plants, Grasses, Sedges and Ferns of Great Britain*. Warne, London, 1891.

Prior, R. C. A. *On the Popular Names of British Plants*. Frederic Norgate, London, 1879.

Radford, E. and M. A. (Ed. Christina Hole) *The Encyclopedia of Superstitions*. Hutchinson, London, 1961.

Ragge, D. R. *Grasshoppers, Crickets and Cockroaches of the British Isles*. Warne, London, 1965.

Reynolds, K. *The Spur Book of Countryside Conservation*. Spurbooks, Edinburgh, 1982.

Sharrock, J. T. R. (Compiler) *The Atlas of Breeding Birds in Britain and Ireland*. Poyser, Berkhamsted, 1977.

Sharrock, J. T. R. *Scarce Migrant Birds in Britain and Ireland*. Poyser, Berkhamsted, 1974.

Shoard, M. *The Theft of the Countryside*. Temple Smith, London, 1980.

South, R. *The Moths of the British Isles*. Warne, London, 1939.

Tansley, A. G. *Britain's Green Mantle*. Allen & Unwin, London, 1968.

Tittensor, A. *The Red Squirrel*. Blandford, Dorset, 1980.

Walters, M. *The Complete Birds of the World*. David & Charles, Newton Abbot, 1980.

Watson, L. *Sea Guide to Whales of the World*. Elsevier-Dutton, New York, USA, 1981.

Wheeler, A. *Fishes of the World*. Ferndale, London, 1979.

White, G. *The Natural History of Selborne*. Whittaker, Treacher, London, 1833.

Whitlock, R. *Historic Forests*. Moonraker, Bradford-on-Avon, Wiltshire, 1979.

Whitlock, R. *Rare and Extinct Birds of Britain*. Phoenix House, London, 1953.

Williams, J. G., Williams, A. E. and Arlott, N. *A Field Guide to the Orchids of Britain and Europe*. Collins, London, 1978.

Woodward, M. (Ed.) *Gerard's Herball*. Gerald Howe, London, 1927.

Photo Credits

Cover: BRUCE COLEMAN Jane Burton (bottom right), John Markham (bottom left); Hans Reinhard (top left); Leonard Lee Rue III (top right).

AGENCE NATURE J. C. Chantelat, page 115; H. Chaumeton, 187 (bottom). S. Andersen 110. Heather Angel, 38, 50, 86. AQUILA PHOTOGRAPHICS Tom Leach 61; John Roberts, 42, 64, 85, 89, 90, 91, 93; D. S. Whitaker, 166. ARDEA LONDON Avon & Tillford 155; M. D. England 163, Bob Gibbons 53, 84; Ake Lindau 94, John Mason, 34, 41, 49, 52, 58, 59, 63, 73, 74, 77, 81, 82, 88, 92, 190 (bottom); Sid Roberts, 119. BIOFOTOS 78; Jeremy Thomas, 184. S. C. Bisserôt 96, 97 (top), 99 (bottom), 100, 101, 103 (bottom), 105 (top). By courtesy of the Trustees, British Museum (Natural History) 188 (top), 189 (top), 192 (centre). BRUCE COLEMAN 127; N. G. Blake, 174; Jane Burton, 98, 104, 105 (bottom), 106, 170, 171, 172, 181; Adrian Davies, 173; L. R. Dawson, 117, 130, 153, 154, 157, 179; Ernest Duscher, 51, 71, 150, 158; Francisco Erize, 108; Michael Freeman, 129; J. L. G. Grande, 99 (top), 102, 143, 191 (bottom); Dennis Green, 121, 122, 124, 134, 142; Pekka Helo, 136; Udo Hirsch, 159, 176; Gordon Langsbury, 147; John Markham, 103 (top), 145,

162, 185; A. J. Mobbs, 175; R. K. Murton, 156; Owen Newman, 180; Chas J. Ott, 45; S. C. Porter, 112, 120, 133; Sandro Prato, 83; Andy Purcell, 146; Hans Reinhard, 46, 65, 68, 69, 70, 97 (bottom), 107, 118, 125, 131, 141, 169, 178, 182, 191 (top); Leonard Lee Rue III, 128, 144; V. Serventy, 160; R. Tidman, 123; J. Tulloch, 167; Derek Washington 72; M. M. Whitehead, 177; Roger Wilmshurt, 126, 135, 148, 149, 151; WWF/J Trotignon, 132; Gunter Ziesler, 140, 152, 161. E. A. Ellis, 183 P. G. H. Evans, 109. Ron & Christine Foord, 39, 40, 43, 44, 57, 66, 67, 75, 76, 80. Andrew N. Gagg, 87. BOB GIBBONS PHOTOGRAPHY Robin Fletcher 60. ERIC & DAVID HOSKING, 116, 137, 138, 139, 164, 165, 168; S. Beaufoy, 186 (top), 187 (top); Ian Rose, 54. Anne Hurst, 192 (top). INSTITUTE OF TERRESTRIAL ECOLOGY Alan Buse, 189 (bottom). Nature Conservancy Council, 37. Peter Wormell, 188 (bottom). NATURE PHOTOGRAPHERS Frank V. Blackburn, 113; Kevin Carlson, 56; Andrew Cleave, 79; Paul Sterry, 55. NHPA Brian Hawkes, 111; R. W. S. Knightsbridge, 186 (bottom). OXFORD SCIENTIFIC FILMS Graham I. Wren, 114. R. J. Pankhurst 35, 36, 47, 48, 62. D. G. Rands, 192 (bottom). Malcolm J. White, 190 (top).

Index

(*Note* This Index does *not* include entries which appear in Notes on the Wildlife and Countryside Act, Natural History and Conservation Organisations and Bibliography.)
Figures in **bold** refer to the illustrated section of the book.